SIMPLE
minds
A Visual Documentary

Omnibus Press LONDON NEW YORK SYDNEY   **mike wrenn**

© Copyright 1990 Omnibus Press
(A Division of Book Sales Limited)

Edited by **Chris Charlesworth**
Book design by **Robert Fairclough**
Cover design by **Liz Nicholson**
Artwork by **Luke Wakeman**
Picture research by **Paul Giblin**
Typesetting and project co-ordination by
Caroline Watson

ISBN 0.7119.2076.1
Order No. OP45640

Exclusive distributors:

Book Sales Limited,
8/9 Frith Street,
London W1V 5TZ, UK.

Music Sales Corporation,
225 Park Avenue South,
New York, NY 10003, USA.

Music Sales Pty Limited,
120 Rothschild Avenue,
Rosebery, NSW 2018, Australia.

To the Music Trade only:
Music Sales Limited,
8/9 Frith Street,
London W1V 5TZ, UK.

Every effort has been made to trace the
copyright holders of the photographs in
this book but one or two were
unreachable. We would be grateful if the
photographers concerned would
contact us.

Typeset by **Capital Setters**, London.
Printed in England by **Ebenezer Baylis
& Son Ltd**, Worcester.

Picture acknowledgements

All Action   p78 (T+B).
Peter Anderson   p24 (C), 25 (L+R), 26,
27 (T+B), 28 (T+B), 30, 31 (B), 62, 63,
64 (T, CL, CR), 68, 69 (L+R).
Santo Basone   p14/5, 16, 18, 19, 20,
21, 24, 29, 31 (T).
Adrian Boot   p3, 40, 42, 43, 44, 45,
46, 47.
George Chin   p67.
London Features Int   Front Cover, 6, 7,
8 (T+B), 9, 12, 32, 34, 35, 36, 37, 38,
39, 48, 52 (L+R), 52/3, 54, 58,
59 (T+B), 60 (T), 61, 73 (T+B), 77 (B),
80, 86 (x4), 88, 89, 90/1 (x5).
Barry Plummer   p50 (T+B), 55 (B).
Pictorial Press   p55, 66, 67, 76,
79 (TL+TR).
Relay Pictures   p56, 77 (T).
Retna   p60 (C+B), 66, 70, 72, 74, 79,
83, 84, 85, 87.
Telegraph Colour Lib   p4.

Omnibus Press is grateful to **Ben Barclay**
and **Mark Longbottom** for the loan of
record sleeves and memorabilia to
illustrate this book.

1 9 7 0 - 1 9 8 9

In a decade of scant musical development, the eighties were no kinder to any progressive band than they were to Simple Minds. Rejected by their first record company, the Scottish troupe steadfastly resisted *most* temptations to play the game.

Instead, they promised to develop their own sound, in their own way, and in their own time. Miraculously, they somehow succeeded.

Simple Minds: A Visual Documentary is an analysis of that achievement, a chronological assessment of the events that led to fame and fortune, as well as a commentary on how it might feel to be part of one of the world's most respected rock bands.

in

the

begin**ning...**

1970

Jim Kerr (singer, lyricist, motivator and self-appointed spokesman of Simple Minds) and Charlie Burchill (guitarist and composer extraordinaire) first meet on a building site at the bottom of Jim's street. They're just eight and seven respectively. Charlie is busy playing in the sand mound, while Jim is already building castles in the sky.

" *I think our backgrounds are a lot to do with everything we're about . . . It's something that's never been talked about before. Our whole thing is because of our backgrounds, because of where we come from, because of our class. The good and the bad. The truths and the hypocrisies. When I was a kid I didn't know what class meant. In Glasgow everybody's the same. There is no class structure, because everybody's working-class. I do remember there being tons and tons of love. Still is. Those people look after each other. Still do. The working classes sort things out.*" **JIM**

" *I love the working classes, but I think they're their own worst enemies. My dad educated himself. He used to work, essentially navvying, and then at night he'd maybe go and see a Shakespearian play. And then he used to go back into work and tell the other guys, and their attitude would be, like, 'Don't try and better yourself.'*" **JIM**

" *I remember moving out of The Gorbals, and into a housing scheme known as the 'new slums', ha! . . . It was a brilliant sense of community there – it's rubbish to say that things like high-rise flats never work. I remember lying in bed as a kid, and it used to be like counting sheep to get to sleep. There were 22 floors in the flats and six houses on every floor, and I knew every family. I used to test myself. You knew pensioners, you knew kids, it was brilliant.*" **JIM**

" *When you're young, you believe in the most basic things. You believe that there are good people around you, and you don't just take things for granted – like the ocean or the sky or even being able to dream, to have a vision, to have ambition. As you grow up all that gets knocked out of you. I remember when I was in school, if you said someone was a dreamer, it was like he was a fool or he didn't get anything done. I don't believe that. And I just started to go much more with what was naturally going through me, as opposed to acting as everyone would expect . . . I think that dreamers are the most powerful people in the world. It's because of dreamers that the world turns.*" **JIM**

" *When you're from the kind of background that we were from, you tend to think that all you're good for is shuffling papers or something like that. If you're going to be an artist of any kind, you have to be from Vienna or somewhere . . .*" **JIM**

OPPOSITE: Street fighting years – Glasgow's Gorbals in the sixties.

FLOWER Power: Peter Gabriel's Genesis provides an early influence.

1973

Jim and Charlie come across a bespectacled Brian McGee at Holyrood Catholic School, in Glasgow. They share an interest in the popular glam-rock movement, and spend many a lunch hour discussing the relative merits of Bowie's lyrics, and Wizard's use of make-up. Jim, rather cruelly, also spends a good deal of time laughing at Brian's specs.

" I remember seeing Brian in the playground with a Wizard key ring and I said, 'Where'd you get that?' And he says, 'I made it.' So I said, 'You gonna make me a Bowie one?' And he did, and he didn't skin me for it. He gave me it for nothing." JIM

" Even before we were really close friends, me and Jim, we'd say hello and talk for five minutes, then we'd see each other at school. Gradually it got to the stage where we'd walk and talk about music. We were in different territories – he lived in high-rise flats, and I lived in maisonette buildings. It was different, but suddenly we realised we had so much in common." CHARLIE

" When I was 14, I used to go to The Citizens' Theatre in Glasgow, where they were really great actors, who could project themselves with one movement. In a theatre you have to know how to throw your personality. I saw how, sometimes, one action or expression can say more than 10 minutes of talk. I think some of that rubbed off on me. But it's funny, I would never dance at school dances. I was always up against the wall, giggling." JIM

" I was always really satisfied up to the age of 15 or 16. I'm the oldest son of three and my parents are really young, so they're also my best friends, that generation gap isn't really there. We were just brought up with traditional values, work hard and you'll get it . . . y'know, determination." JIM

1974

Genesis release their last recorded work with Peter Gabriel. An adventurous double album called 'The Lamb Lies Down on Broadway', it has an overwhelming influence on the three friends, who all start dreaming of a career in music.

" I can remember really enjoying the learning process of music. My mum bought me a guitar with 3,500 cigarette coupons, and I taught myself with the help of a John Mayall record we had lying around. And even though I really hate John Mayall, it was a start . . ." CHARLIE

" Our school was Catholic, and I used to totally believe in it all. And then I began to get these feelings that there was something queer about a God based on fear, that God will punish you if you do this or that. I just thought, 'What kind of a God could it be that punishes anybody?' I was 15 then, and going to church suddenly became so unspiritual. My ma would say, 'You'd better go to church now,' and my dad would say, 'Ah, it's crap all that.' Our house was like that though – a picture of Christ on one wall, a picture of Lenin on another, and a picture of John Kennedy on another." JIM

1976

Jim quits school during the summer, and immediately finds work as an apprentice engineer. He doesn't enjoy the job however, and looks to music as a way out. With Charlie and Brian sharing his frustration, the trio decide to form a group — Johnny And The Self Abusers.

" *When we first left school, Charlie and I hitch-hiked around Britain and Europe, ending up in Milan with no money. I remember lying in the fields there and looking at the sky, hoping it wouldn't rain. It was then that we started the band 'cause, like, futures and careers didn't count any more. It was the breaking of ties . . . emancipation. We felt that, if we could do all this, then . . .* " JIM

" *Glasgow's a funny city to start a musical career . . . It's the sort of place where being a hairdresser is about the only form of self expression. If people asked what you did and you said, 'I write words,' they'd say, 'Are you queer? Are you weird?'* " JIM

" *I used to go to gigs dressed up in the whole glam thing – big boots, mascara, painted nails. Next day I'd be working on my building site, trying to get enough money to go hitch-hiking round Europe, and I'd notice I'd still got a trace of nail varnish on. And I'd be terrified these giants, these bears that I worked with, would discover it. Other than that, of course, I was perfectly normal.* " JIM

" *The first gig I ever saw was Genesis, when Gabriel was in the band. I really liked the presence of him especially. His approach to things was pretty intense. One minute he could be some monster, then the next, soft and gentle. The bit in between was unnerving because I couldn't decide whether he was a headbanger, or totally sane. It was never far out hippy stuff, there was always a menace in what he did.* " JIM

ROY Wood's Wizzard.

THE raw energy of The Sex
Pistols and the punk movement
inspired Johnny And The Self
Abusers. Below: their first
single sleeve.

*" We might have enjoyed a lot of the mid-seventies music but, let's be honest,
if it wasn't for punk, we would never have got going – we just wouldn't
have known where to start. That was the great thing about what punk had
done. It had given everyone a chance – even us."* BRIAN

1977

february

Quickly developing into a seven-piece outfit, the Glaswegian group retain an interest in
the glam-rock sound, though now model themselves on those profitable punk
stereotypes of the period. And although the somewhat excessive line-up of three
guitars, bass, drums and saxophone might seem incongruous, their early gigs at the
Doune Castle pub and Zhivago's Disco go down a storm.

march

The band buy their first tour bus, for just £350. A battered vehicle that used to belong to
a local school for the mentally handicapped, the lads persuade their parents to chip in
50 quid each. They then pay back the debt, to the tune of three pounds a week each.

april

Johnny And The Self Abusers develop their act with twin vocalists. The *other* one is a
bloke called John Milarky, noted primarily for his fairly riotous manner of performance,

as well as for a song he wrote during this period, called 'Pablo Picasso'. The lyrics go something like this: 'Pablo Picasso, all the girls think you're an asshole . . .' He was clearly heavily influenced by John Cale or Jonathan Richman.

october

Following a string of regular bookings at Glasgow's claustrophobic Mars Bar Club, Johnny And The Self Abusers begin to make a name for themselves with their Sex Pistols covers, Ray Davies rewrites (!) and Velvet Underground rip-offs. In consequence, they're invited to sign a contract with London's ambitious Chiswick Records. Ill feeling is already running high however, with the group showing signs of a distinct lack of unity. The working-class element, Jim, Charlie, and Brian, are increasingly at odds with the other members who, coincidentally or otherwise, all stem from wealthier roots.

november

The band's first single is released. Entitled 'Saints And Sinners', it isn't received well by the music press. "They have a great name, but the song doesn't do much," says *Sounds*. "A futile thrashing of pseudopunk, Bowie colliding with Ferry," reckons the *NME*. "Relentlessly rank and file," claims *Melody Maker*. The critics are aiming at an invisible target however. By now, Johnny And The Self Abusers have already split up. Milarky and Co. set off to form Cuban Heels, while the others, er, don't.

december

Determined to develop their dream of a musical career, Jim, Charlie and Brian decide to launch a new venture, this time with a keyboard player. Unfortunately no one replies to their advertisement, so they take a second guitarist instead — one Duncan Barnwell.

LOU Reed, the band's all American hero.

" *Although we were in with things that were happening around the punk scene, what with our name and everything, we were doing stuff off Doctors Of Madness albums. It was always on that level, rather than singing about riots and daft things like that.*" JIM

" *Almost on a parallel with the boogie bands, the punks did that exact same speed of number – guaranteed to shock and get people going. And that really isn't the function of music. So much of the punk era was a political movement. It got to the stage where guys were singing about nine-to-five jobs and life on the dole, and it was really boring. Just saying, 'I'm bored, full stop,' didn't appeal to me.*" CHARLIE

" *There was always an art thing in us. We wanted to get a band along those lines of darkness, and a sort of awareness, and put it over in an attractive type of art package. We wanted a band that could project.*" JIM

" *We knew things couldn't go on with Johnny And The Self Abusers. So finally, the unsatisfactory element left, and the good element went on to form Simple Minds.*" CHARLIE

S m

DAVID Bowie: "She's so simple minded."

1978

january

The quartet call themselves Simple Minds (after a line in David Bowie's 'Jean Genie') and immediately start rehearsing in a local lampshade factory. On the 18th they play their first ever gig, supporting Steel Pulse at Satellite City, a disco perched above Glasgow's Apollo Theatre. Tony Donald (a former Self Abuser) stands in on bass, while a new Gaelic recruit named Mick MacNeil shows what he can do with his keyboards.

march

Tony Donald quits, and Simple Minds are finally augmented with bassist Derek Forbes. Hot-foot from a line-up calling itself The Subs, Derek comes to Simple Minds with fascinating credentials. Seems he's spent most of his working life playing bass in Spanish dance bands, but has also been involved with a more progressive outfit called Big Dick And The Four Skins. A friend of Barnwell's however, Derek is readily forgiven.

may

The band record their first demo tape, at Glasgow's Ca Va Studios. It features six songs, 'Act Of Love', 'Chelsea Girl', 'Wasteland', 'Did You Ever', 'Cocteau Twins' and 'Pleasantly Disturbed'. It costs the group just £226 to record, and is later described by *ZigZag*'s Lindsay Hutton as one of the greatest demos ever!

june

Simple Minds and Duncan Barnwell part company. Charlie explains that the second guitarist isn't really needed.

july

Simple Minds make the big trip to London, but can't impress any record companies. The major labels seem too scared to commit themselves, since none of their recent signings are taking off. So the boys try one or two minor companies *including* Zoom. They turn them down too.

august

Back in Scotland, the group make their Edinburgh début, opening for Billy Idol's Generation X. Watched by a local fanzine writer, Brian Hogg, Simple Minds put on a dazzling display and are immediately recommended to Hogg's friend, record shop manager and Zoom Records' supremo, Bruce Findlay. In consequence, Bruce goes to see Simple Minds and then spends the rest of the year trying to establish both recording and managerial contracts with the group.

Over the ensuing months, a series of deals will eventually be struck with both Zoom and their parent company, Arista Records. Findlay finally manages to attract the band to his

label, on the strict understanding that Arista will meet all major financial demands of the outfit. Indeed, it's reported that Simple Minds do rather well out of the arrangement, benefiting from a load of new equipment, as well as a year's wage being met for the whole group. Needless to say, full recording costs are on the house as well, *and* the group get their first professional publicist — one Brian Hogg!

october

By now Simple Minds are beginning to impress the critics as well as the money men. In an autumn review, *NME* scribe and Simple Minds' 'friend' Ian Cranna writes: "You know that band that everybody's been waiting for — the one that will achieve that magical fusion of the verbal visions of the Bowie/Harley/Verlaine twilight academy with the fertile firepower of the new wave, that early Roxy Music with a rock and roll heart? Well, here they are . . ."

december

Simple Minds decline a series of requests to move to London. They feel their family and musical roots are in Scotland, and justifiably resent any implication that they *need* to be in the capital. A second demo tape produces the tracks 'Someone' and 'Sad Affair', along with enough new ideas to suggest they're more than ready to record their first album.

" *J*oining Simple Minds was really quite a strange step for me to take . . . I'd actually started out playing the accordion when I was nine. I formed a band with my brother Danny, and we just used to play at local dances. We were called The Barnets, and we even got on TV – on a show called Junior Showtime. I had to wear a kilt and, for the next year at school, I walked around with a permanent red face." MICK

" *A* lot of people think we've had it really easy because we didn't work the London club circuit . . . y'know, they didn't see us at the Hope And Anchor. And to be honest, we would rather have gone out and got a grass roots following. But we also wanted to get things straight. We wanted a proper studio, a proper sound, a proper producer. And obviously we couldn't have done that on our own." JIM

" *I* don't know what would have become of me if Simple Minds hadn't got that initial deal . . . I remember I had to go to an interview for the Civil Service in Glasgow, because the dole wouldn't give me any more money. There were over 30 people trying for the job, and I tried my hardest to fail. I went in like a real mess, completely dishevelled, and put on this whole act like I was completely untogether. A week later they wrote back to me and said, 'You were great, you've got the job.' And the job was a refuse collector. Luckily at that time there was a lot of interest in the band and we got a deal. Otherwise, I don't know what I would have done." JIM

CRITICS claimed 'Life In A Day' echoed the sound of early Roxy Music.

january

The band invite their choice of producer, John Leckie, to see them play a gig at Dundee University. Leckie, who'd masterminded the first Magazine LP, 'Real Life', and who'd also worked with one of Charlie's favourite bands, Doctors Of Madness, is bowled over by what he hears. Not unnaturally, acquaintances of the band are impressed by this new connection. It was Leckie who, as a recording engineer, had worked with Phil Spector on The Beatles' legendary 'Let It Be' album.

february

Simple Minds start work on their first LP, at Farmyard Studios in Amersham.

march

They appear on television for the first time. Featured on Annie Nightingale's revamped *Old Grey Whistle Test*, Scotland's local heroes are presented as international stars of the future. 'Life In A Day', the title track from their now completed album, is released as their début single for Zoom.

april

Bruce Findlay starts work as the group's official manager. At the same time Arista's Business Affairs Manager, Robert White, appears to become Findlay's partner. The group hit the road on a massive promotional tour, supporting Howard Devoto's Magazine.

Halfway through the UK trek Simple Minds' début album, 'Life In A Day', is unleashed to mixed reviews. *NME*'s Tony Stewart is already a big fan however, and refers to them as ". . . redefining the new sound of the seventies, which gives so much hope for rock 'n' roll in the eighties. Simple Minds are one of the few bands to draw on the strings of the early to mid-seventies, and construct an accessible and commercial formula."

In view of their fast-growing status, Simple Minds are quickly offered a new agency deal – and a major publishing contract. The single peaks at 62 in the UK chart.

SIMPLE Minds, circa 1979. Clockwise: Jim Kerr, Brian McGee, Derek Forbes, Mick McNeil and Charlie Burchill.

may

After a successful climax to their promotional trip with Magazine (Simple Minds stole the show at London's Theatre Royal, Drury Lane), the Scottish troupe set out for their own tour of the country's smaller venues. The response is slightly disappointing.

EARLY gig at London's Marquee
with Charlie interchanging
guitar and violin.

june

A second single, 'Chelsea Girl', becomes available. Some critics call it innovative, which makes Jim laugh, since he openly admits to stealing the riff from a track called 'Temporary Thing' on Lou Reed's 'Rock 'n' Roll Heart' album.

august

Increasingly scornful of their vinyl product to date, Simple Minds are keen to get back into the studio to make amends. Again with John Leckie at the helm, the band start work on their second LP at Rockfield Studios in Monmouth. In search of their own 'sound', the band refuse to play any of the LP live until it's completed. As a result the record will be completely studio conceived.

september

While recording at Rockfield, Simple Minds bump into David Bowie and Iggy Pop who are working on the latter's current album, 'Soldier', in the studio next door. The band are flattered to be invited to provide backing vocals on the Bowie-penned 'Play It Safe', and duly oblige.

october

The second album finished, Simple Minds head out on the road to promote their new work. In addition to a series of UK dates, the band also make their first brief visits to Europe and the States, going down especially well at New York's Hurrah Club.

december

'Real To Real Cacophony' is finally released, seemingly against the wishes of their record company. Arista make little secret of their disappointment in Simple Minds' new material, which they see as commercial suicide, and friction begins to set in. Keeping cool throughout it all, the band seem greatly developed when they appear on *The Old Grey Whistle Test*, and John Peel's prestigious radio show. The year ends with a show at Glasgow Technical College.

" *People say we're deliberately weird. But we're not trying to be – although we're no Joe Ordinaries either. It would be easy to be weird for the sake of it, but that is the easy way out. We try hard to put soul and feeling into every song that we do. Passion is important to move people. And there is a lot of humour in our songs."* JIM

" *Critics look at us, and groups like us, and say we're 'Art School' rock. Art school rock! We're fucking closer to bricklayers and plumbers. It's just stupid. They say we're Moderne lads with silly eye mascara, making pointless cold music – all alienated and everything. I should fucking well think we do feel alienated, coming from the Gorbals where, if you aren't totally into football and girls, there's really something the matter with you – and where it's really difficult for you to get involved with anything like music . . . I wish there was a decent title, much as I don't like them, for bands like Roxy, Magazine and us. Like when you get two R&B bands, you don't compare the sound, you look at them both and that's R&B. There should be a reasonable title to use."* JIM

" *Speaking musically, I think everything that is going to be done, has been done within the confines of musical notes. So what I feel you have to do is sort of stretch people's imagination, to open up. It's like escapism really."* CHARLIE

" *This kind of music takes your mind further out. It's trying to take steps ahead in rock music generally, into unknown areas. For example, when listening to Eno, you suddenly realise he's taking steps out there. Compare it to the desert. Nothing happens out there, no one wants to go out there, and it's the same with music. There are areas where no one will go near, they feel it's too unappealing or too unusual. They feel uncomfortable. This type of music moves out there.*" JIM

" *It was so ham fisted . . . The 'Life In A Day' album came in at number 32, the single was like 68, and Arista had these big ads saying, 'Hit single, hit album.' In fact, we got that high in the chart with comparatively low sales, simply because nothing else was happening in the music scene.*" JIM

" *We feel really restricted in Glasgow. There isn't anywhere for us to play because of size, organisation and that kind of thing. We played a college gig a while back, it was a tiny little hall and there were five hundred people in it and no bouncers anywhere. It was bedlam.*" CHARLIE

" *I don't really enjoy playing Glasgow. It's a weird place for a band at our stage. When you first start off, everyone in Glasgow gets right behind you. But there isn't much going on in Glasgow, so when you get a band that's getting on a bit, everybody really gets jealous. It's like, 'Those up there, those cunts. It could've been me.'*" JIM

" *When we begin a show, it's a menacing thing. It's intimidating, as if we're taking a stand against the audience. It's a case of projecting yourself above them, ultimately for them to enjoy it. People think it's an arrogant pose but, er, it isn't really.*" JIM

" *Two months after 'Life In A Day' came out, we were really embarrassed by it. It was very, very poppy, and we realised we were drowned in influence. We had to try to get our own sound . . . We had to stop messing about.*" JIM

" *We told Arista we'd got all these great songs for the second album, and they said, 'OK do them.' But when we played them they said, 'What's this?' So we showed them the cover – just plain blue – and they said, 'It's horrible!' They went, 'Jesus, where's the 'Chelsea Girl'?' And we said, 'Well, there isn't one . . .'*" JIM

" *With 'Real To Real Cacophony', we didn't demo anything before we went into the studio. All we had were cassettes with little bits on. We just went in and did it, and that's going to be our attitude from now on. On edge, where you have to make spot decisions. It wasn't safe, and that felt good. We knew we had to get a sound of our own. We talked with John Leckie about what we wanted, and we questioned everything, even in the vocals. On the first album they were so held back, bland and smooth. But this time I just wrote everything down, sat back for half an hour and worked it all out. Then I'd go in and say, 'Right, let's do it,' and catch the spontaneous feel. That's where it all comes from.*" JIM

" *I won't believe we've really cracked it, until we can be known just as The Minds – the same way that The Rolling Stones are now universally accepted as The Stones.*" JIM

january

**A** new single, 'Changeling', taken from 'Real to Real Cacophony', is released.

february

Constantly at loggerheads with the powers that be at Arista, Bruce Findlay's Zoom operation finally folds. This doesn't directly affect Simple Minds however, since the band are already contracted to the parent company in a separate deal.

Meanwhile, the band follow-up their earlier, rather promising trip to Europe, with a much more substantial tour (at one point they support Gary Numan on some of his dates). The experience has a tremendous impact on all concerned, and will prove an unbridled influence upon their next collection of songs.

may

Back at Rockfield, again with Leckie, Simple Minds start their new work.

september

The third album, 'Empires And Dance' is released. A more political offering than previous efforts, the LP is specifically dance orientated and supposedly — or so say the music press — wholly representative of a 'New European' movement in contemporary song writing. Most people who buy it just like the tunes however, and the album reaches 41 in the chart. It probably would have sold quicker however, if the record company had pressed more than 7,500 copies at a time.

The single plucked from said album, 'I Travel', becomes an immediate dance floor hit. Which is to say, it gets played in clubs quite a bit, but nobody buys it.

The group find themselves desperately broke, and can't see the situation changing while they're still with Arista.

october

With their shows starting to attract larger and more appreciative audiences though, Simple Minds are beginning to earn attention from their peers. One of the biggest stars to be impressed by the band's sound is former Genesis leader, Peter Gabriel, who now invites the impoverished Scots to accompany him on a European tour. Interestingly, this will be the trek that introduces a new song, 'Biko', to Gabriel's Continental audience.

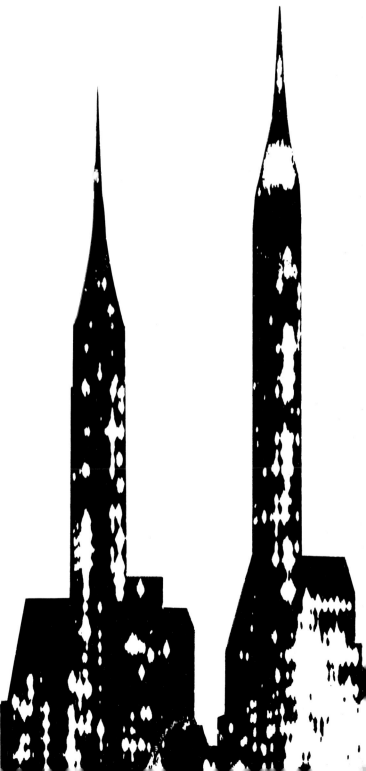

november

With Gabriel reportedly paying Simple Minds' expenses (some claim it's his record company footing the bill), the band get the chance to revisit familiar haunts — as well as discovering new ones in places such as Portugal, Greece and Italy.
On the German leg, Derek Forbes becomes something of a hero when he saves the life of a Düsseldorf man in the street near the venue. Seemingly dead in the gutter, the local resident responds favourably to the bass player's attempts at heart massage. Nobody is more surprised than Derek.

" *We do run a giant risk of being labelled as pretentious, being Glasgow boys and singing about Europe. But you can't blind yourself and pretend that nothing exists outside your home town. We're not trying to solve the problems of the world or anything like that, but we are showing that we don't just sit in the recording studio and assume that there's nothing happening in the outside world.* " JIM

" *We were driving through East Germany, and it was like going from a colour picture into black and white, no neon lights for 60 miles. Just before you go into the Western sector of Berlin, there are these Russian tanks, troops and missiles everywhere. Even through a van window, how can you not be affected by something like that?* " JIM

" *The idea of a Moscow dominated world really freaks me out. But a Los Angeles dominated world frightens me every bit as much. Maybe I should be writing about life in the disco or something, but then I pick up the paper and read that every house in Switzerland has an in-built fucking fall-out shelter! You can't ignore things like that. With lyrics, sometimes you say something and you think it's really yucky and pretentious. There's words like 'war' — I'd never used them, they're so strong. But when you go and see things, it's even more pretentious to think everything is safe.* " JIM

" *'Travel' is an important development for us . . . If we can do a song that's appealing, but with an edge so it doesn't get too comfortable, people might listen to what's being said.* " JIM

" *Once you get behind a microphone you have a degree of power, and people look up to you. But then you get stuff that is really condescending, like telling you how bad war is. I mean big deal. Everyone knows that.* " JIM

" *I think we're a bit vague in a way. I don't think we've yet put our head on a block and said, 'This is fact!' Because I don't think we know anything as 100 per cent fact. I mean, political wise, there are plenty of good themes for songs, but who really knows who is right?* " JIM

" *At times I feel dead guilty mentioning anything political, because I don't vote, and you know what a waste of time that is. But I'm not going to vote until I've done enough research into it.* " JIM

" *'Thirty Frames A Second' was a lot heavier when I wrote it. It was about a man who becomes a father, but he no longer recognises his children because they haven't made the same mistakes that he did. They reject his food*

and everything. But it turns out to be the song of a man looking back, trying to grasp what purpose there is in existing." JIM

" **T**he songs are just an attempt to educate myself, to get to grips with what's going on." JIM

" **P**eople start labelling things as 'European', and they have only a really vague idea of what they mean by it. In Germany or Holland, the whole musical idea of 'The Europeans' means nothing. It doesn't even exist! The only people to whom that whole thing exists, are the readers of the British music papers." CHARLIE

" **I** had a kind of argument with Richard Jobson (with The Skids at this time), who said we were betraying our heritage by playing all this funk, black and European music. He said we should be getting a young sound of Scotland going. I was saying that we just don't get any heather and stuff in Glasgow. We're from a different part of Scotland to The Skids . . . when I first met them I couldn't understand a word they were saying, their accents were so thick!" JIM

" **P**eople make too much of where a group comes from. They expect us to be very Scottish, very patriotic and proud of our roots . . . and because we come from Glasgow, they expect us to be even more like that. But I think it alienates people if you play too much on it. If people start liking various groups just because they come from Sheffield or Liverpool, it gets like football. Well, music is about sound, isn't it? It's about heart. It's not about what's happening in the background or what's behind it. It's something that provokes a reaction!" JIM

" **W**hen I see Gabriel now, I can't see it from the outside. I still retain the excitement of being a small boy watching him front Genesis. And I'm still in awe of him. He still has integrity. So many bands today give the impression that they'd rather take pictures of a man getting beat up in the street, than actually try to help him. 'Biko' might drown in its art, but it still draws attention to its subject." JIM

" **W**e thought we'd just be dropped by Arista. But when it came to the crunch . . . we got some good reviews for 'Empires And Dance', and we were getting a bit of reaction in Europe, so they weren't prepared to let us go as easily as we'd hoped. We were well sick." JIM

" **W**e worked really hard on 'Empires And Dance'. I remember doing the backing track for 'Capital City', and just keeping on going 'till we'd finished – at gone five in the morning. I remember we all crashed out, went to bed, whatever, and didn't get up for another 24 hours. We were that shattered." BRIAN

" **W**e're only in debt through trying to make things better for the group, getting out of the contract and making sure we've got the best possible equipment and the best instruments and everything. The only thing we've been guilty of is making a substandard first album." JIM

january

Simple Minds return for a British tour, which they hope will take them another rung up the ladder. Not this time though. After playing to 40,000 every night in Europe, the band are back to 200 kids in Scunthorpe. Jim is appalled, not least because it appears the record company have made no effort to promote the shows. Brian McGee threatens to quit and, eventually, the tail-end of the tour is scrapped anyway, as the band return to Glasgow to rehearse some new material.

february

Threatening to sack their manager, Simple Minds doggedly pursue their freedom from Arista Records who, extraordinary as it may seem, now decide they want to keep the group after all. In turn, the band soon decide they want to keep their manager too, especially since Findlay is doing his best to set up a new deal with Virgin Records. At last reaching the end of their current contract, Simple Minds agree to forgo any further royalties on their first three albums, in order to meet debts they've incurred during their time with Arista. The business relationship is now over, and the band throw themselves at the mercy of Richard Branson's Virgin Records. Branson himself greets the group with open arms, and agrees to meet them for a welcoming lunch at Glasgow's Albany Hotel. The band play the new boss a tape of their latest songs. It includes rough 'n' ready mixes of 'Love Song', 'The American', 'Sweat In Bullet' and 'League Of Nations'. Branson loves them, and everyone goes home happy.

march

By way of celebration, the boys play a couple of shows in Glasgow and London, receiving an enthusiastic response from critics and punters alike. Then it's off on a short US Club tour. The tour ends up briefer than planned however, with Brian McGee falling foul of nervous exhaustion, and having to return home before the dates can be completed. A projected UK and European itinerary is subsequently scrapped.

april

Back in Britain, Simple Minds again find themselves at Farmyard Studios. This time though, they're without John Leckie. Their new material is being produced by former Gong guitarist, Steve Hillage — famed for his lifelong obsession with woolly hats and flying teapots. An innovative eccentric, Hillage keeps a potted plant in the studio, so he's always got 'someone' to talk to when the band aren't around! Everyone agrees Steve to be a 'nice bloke', but he's fairly new to the production game, and his inexperience soon begins to tell. Unable to control the band's working methods, they all end up with too much to do, in too short a time — though they *eventually* get a result.

THE 'Sons And Fascination' tour visits Liverpool.

may

Simple Minds' first single for Virgin, 'The American', is released. It makes it to number 59, and will eventually find a home on 'Sister Feelings Call'.

july

With recording commitments finally completed, and signs that Simple Minds are about to enter an especially busy promotional period, Brain McGee announces his plans to leave the group. He's never liked travelling and, with the promise of a busy autumn on the way, decides he's finally had enough. The split is completely amicable, and the outfit look to an old friend, Kenny Hyslop, to stand in for forthcoming live commitments. For his part, Kenny is relieved to find an escape route from his current position of employ. One-time percussionist with fellow Zoom signing, The Zones, Kenny has recently been working with Richard Jobson's group, The Skids. The down-to-earth camaraderie of Simple Minds, seems like a breath of fresh air after the sterility of a Skids rehearsal.

august

Having ended up with too much material for the new LP, Simple Minds can't decide what to discard. So in the end, they choose to keep the lot and release two albums together as a limited edition. No one wants it marketed as a 'double album', so 'Sons And Fascination' is sold with 'Sister Feelings Call' offered as a 'free gift'. Released slightly ahead of schedule, the set immediately enters the chart at 14, and finally peaks at 11. 'Love Song' is plucked from 'Sons' as the next single. It makes it to 47 in the UK. The band preview their new material at a one-off show in Edinburgh, as part of the city's annual Arts Festival.

september

The 'double album' is repackaged into two separate sleeves, with 'Sons And Fascination' emerging this month, and 'Sister Feelings Call' the next.
The band confirm a series of dates abroad, and bid Britain farewell with a string of shows at Nottingham, Glasgow, Manchester, Newcastle, Liverpool and London. They also replace The Cure (who have extended their Canadian tour) at Stafford's Futurama Festival.

october

After a brief excursion to Canada and the States, Simple Minds follow stablemates Magazine and XTC to Australia, and are quick to imitate their success. Supporting Aussie hit-makers Icehouse, The Minds win enough native support to try out a few dates on their own, all of which go down a storm. By the time they leave, 'Love Song' is already in the Top 10.

november

'Sweat In Bullet' becomes the third and final hit single from the double package. It peaks at 52.

" *Some journalist said it was a contradiction to have a dance beat with something totally different on top of it. He liked 'Empires And Dance', but said it was like doing a Charleston into the Third Reich or something. Like, we're trying to point out some problems, but we're taking a kind of evasive path. Then what happens, is that people who are generally a bit gullible put things into a category like, 'doomy depressive thing', or 'high joyful thing'. We definitely take the same routes as other bands. You go to a record company and they take your product to a radio show and try to get it on. We're definitely as much a rock band as anyone. But I hate using words like 'gigs'. If you make an album once every 10 months, you want as many people as possible to hear it. There's nothing better than getting a letter from the other side of the world.*" JIM

" *We wanted a change from John Leckie, purely because we wanted to see what the difference was. We heard this track by Ken Lockie (another Virgin artist) and it sounded amazing. We asked who'd produced it, and they said it was Steve Hillage.*" CHARLIE

" *We'd never heard any Steve Hillage work before, but I knew Steve's image – y'know, ol' cabbage head – and there was obviously a giant contrast with ours. But we met him, and he was talking about a lot of European bands – Can and Neu – and it just seemed we had that in common.*" JIM

" *Steve actually fell out of his seat one time. There were some steps that you had to climb before you could get to the mixing desk, and he used to sit up there, in this swivel chair, and totally lose himself in his work. And he always played everything real loud, so he'd really be in his own world, with all these funny habits, like picking his nose and scratching his balls and stuff. And one night he got himself in his usual trance, went to swivel round in his chair and that was it – he fell out, toppled down the stairs, and just lie there going, 'Bastard! Fucking stairs!' Ha-ha! And this is all, like, halfway through the mix, so he had to climb the stairs, plonk himself back down in his seat, and start again. Classic. Fucking classic.*" CHARLIE

" *I think Hillage was freaked by the amount of work we took upon ourselves. We hadn't got too well organised, none of us had planned what we would be doing or how it would fit on the record. And if the producer and the band are unprepared for the job in hand, then it's always gonna be a stressful exercise – which it was.*" MICK

" **Y**ou haven't lived until you've been in a car with Hillage, he's hilarious. He'd be driving round town and stuff, and whenever he'd see a policeman on a bike, he'd slow right down, wind down his window, and shout out 'Go home you cunt.' Somehow he seemed to get away with it." CHARLIE

" **W**e were changing direction during our first album for Virgin. To try and get everything onto one album, would have put the whole thing out of focus. We could have scrapped tracks, but we had spent money on them, and we were proud of them, so in the end, we talked to the record company, and agreed to put out two albums. It isn't really a double, we just put them together as a kind of gift." JIM

" **I**'m pleased with the set, although I do feel it's a tiny bit one-paced and samey. The only thing we were disappointed in, was the production at times. Whereas with 'Empires And Dance' there was novelty in the production, 'Sons And Fascination' was much more traditional, and we didn't really see that happening. But some of the feeling in it was really good. There was a lot of beauty." JIM

" **T**he lyrics are a collage. I don't sit down and just write songs and verses. I'm constantly writing and adding things, taking lines that have been written over a period of a year and piecing them together. One line can be

the image of a song, and the rest can be padding. If it came to a lyric sheet, I'd now rather take a line from each song. I think you'd get more of a focus. It's becoming more of a schizophrenic thing. Of course the lyrics are very important but, in terms of value and that, I wouldn't care if no one at all paid any attention. They're all pictures in themselves, every line's a different picture. It's the atmosphere of words. It could be for the sound, or it could be for the meaning, or for the image of the word. They deal with a lot of images and ambiguities." JIM

"**B**oys From Brazil' *isn't about the Ira Levin book, although that was a starting point. Rather than find a base line like 'Death to the Neo-Nazis', we wanted to be ambiguous. It was just a point, a motivation. It's a game we play, and when it comes to lyrics, I think we're too scared to commit ourselves. That song was concerned with seeing, in Britain, that almost total Neo-Nazi romance, which is really dangerous.*" JIM

"**W**e wrote 'Sons' *in America, but recorded it in Britain when the riots were going on. People said, 'Oh this is really unexpected,' but we knew it was coming. It had followed us everywhere – the Munich bomb disaster, street riots in Amsterdam, Italy, Belgium. It just goes to show the attitude of people here who're content to think they're the centre of the world.*" JIM

" **M**y eyes hit on things and I have to say them. I thought America was all Fourth Avenue and Cadillacs but, when we were there, it was a really anxious time. The hostages had just been released, the key word was heroes. But those people weren't heroes, they were just victims of circumstances who had survived." JIM

" **A** newsflash came on saying Reagan had been shot. I jumped out of bed, put on some clothes, and dashed down to the bar to get some drinks. And there were all these Italians there, cheering and celebrating because they thought he'd been bumped off. It would have made a brilliant film . . . I can't let situations like that go to waste." JIM

" **W**e've been accused of making hollow travel music, but we're not sending postcards from exotic places. There's a lot more to us than that. If it was hollow travel music, we'd probably have hit singles. As it is, our singles don't get played enough for that to happen. We're not going to be a constant source of documentaries or travelogues, our music is always changing. I think the reason we don't get played more is that the music shocks them too much. There's too much passion in it, and that makes people uncomfortable." JIM

" **W**e're packing out big halls, but we haven't had to cheapen our music to get vital airplay. We haven't had to do arrangements we didn't want to, we haven't had to attach ourselves to any category or movement simply because it is currently fashionable. We're still really vulnerable. We dislike people who don't like our music, but we don't believe people who really do like it. We want to know why they like it." JIM

" **I** think if I was totally concerned with the problems of the world, I'd be a missionary or something, as opposed to working for Virgin Records." JIM

" **I**t's a compliment to say we sound like a Virgin band in one way, but of course it's crap as well. I don't like our new sleeve because I think it looks very Virginy but, on the other hand, I'm glad our stuff's getting sold with The Human League etc, as opposed to James Last or Barry Manilow." JIM

" **I**f you went to see The Skids you'd get all these guys in the audience shouting for 'Albert Tatlock' and Jobson would come out with something like that 'Dulce Et Decorum Est' instead. One minute he's Nicky Tesco, the next he's Jean Paul Sartre." CHARLIE

" **B**efore we went to Australia, I thought it was going to be really bland. But it's actually a lot more creative than people realise. Sydney's probably going to be the next Hollywood." CHARLIE

" **K**enny Hyslop hasn't actually joined us. We like him a lot, but he's got his fingers in lots of different pies. I don't think we will try and get a permanent drummer. Brian was the only drummer I've ever played with. It'll be hard for anyone coming in new, and it'll be hard for us as well because we're used to each other, our sense of humour. I think we'll just leave it until the touring's over and see what happens." JIM

" **Y**ou know, we never really thought about selling records until we saw the size of our debts." JIM

january

Simple Minds book into a studio for 10 days, for the sole purpose of working out and rehearsing some new numbers. One particular tune, 'Promised You A Miracle', develops quicker than any other and, frightened of losing the *feel* of it, they decide to put it onto tape there and then. It's Hyslop's first recording with the band, and will prove to be his last.

february

Arista Records decide to cash in on Simple Minds' increasing popularity and rush release 'Celebration' — an album of old material, still owned by the band's former label. The move will later provoke Virgin to purchase all rights to their earlier work.

For their part, the group are already engaged on another round of shows in Europe. Sweden, Holland, Germany, France, Belgium . . . making new friends all the time.

april

'Promised You A Miracle' is released, and makes the usual crawl to the lower reaches of the Top 50.

may

Out of the blue, or so it seems to the teen press, the single shoots up the chart to number 13. It's their first *real* hit single, and the band dash back to London to make their début on *Top Of The Pops*.

june

Recording now with deadlines in mind, the group plough through their sessions with a change of drummers. After Hyslop's departure (he returns to his own band, Set The Tone) a former Café Jacques percussionist, Mike Ogletree, joins up for a while. He's *technically* brilliant, but doesn't seem to have the right kind of welly. So instead, a south Londoner named Mel Gaynor is enlisted to help finish the new album. Having ventured to play with a true diversity of modern bands — from the metallic Samson to the positively funky Linx — Mel provides Simple Minds with a much more substantial foundation on which to build their new sounds. In return, Kerr and Co. keep Mel in beer money for as long as he wants the gig. By the time the band play Britain in the autumn, Mel will have made the seat his own.

july

Simple Minds play a couple of club dates in Glasgow and Manchester. They also appear on the same bill as Peter Gabriel and Echo And The Bunnymen at this year's Bath Festival, near Shepton Mallet.

august

A world tour gets under way, with a series of festival appearances all over Europe. 'Glittering Prize' is released as their tenth single to date. It makes it to 16 in the chart.

september

The album, 'New Gold Dream (81-82-83-84)', at last reaches the shops. Simple Minds had wanted it produced by Steve Lillywhite, but he couldn't fit them into his schedule. Instead, a talented studio engineer by the name of Peter Walsh takes the credit. The songs, incidentally, are no longer attributed to individual writers. Now, the whole band is to be responsible for every song – and the material is labelled accordingly. Simple Minds play the Edinburgh Festival, again.

MEL Gaynor, the full time replacement for Brian McGee.

october

'New Gold Dream (81-82-83-84)' peaks at three in the LP chart, and gives the group their first ever gold disc. They celebrate by returning to the road, on a journey which will take them across Australia and Canada, before returning home for the UK leg.

november

'Someone Somewhere In Summertime' becomes the third single from the latest album, and is destined to be the worst seller, reaching only 36 in the home chart. Meanwhile, the band meet their UK commitments, with shows in Glasgow, Newcastle, Belfast, Dublin, Leeds, Manchester, Liverpool and Cardiff.

december

The tour continues at Exeter, Oxford, Brighton, Ipswich, Norwich, London, Stoke, Birmingham, Leicester, Sheffield, Derby, Bristol, Dundee, Aberdeen and Edinburgh. Simple Minds finally come to rest with a Christmas show at Glasgow's Tiffany's.

" *We played 'Promised You A Miracle' for about an hour in rehearsal, thought it sounded good, then went on to something else. But later that night it was going round and round in our heads so we thought we'd just do it, not get precious about it, just see what happened.* " JIM

" *We've never thought about hit singles until very recently. That's because we feel capable of it now. We didn't form the band to have hit singles and gold albums. We wanted to find a sound with an international appeal.*

At Arista I thought we were really doomed to be a cult. I believed all the press wrote about us being cold, bleak and industrial. That bothered us because we were making music that deserved to be heard." CHARLIE

" *I think that before, when you heard our singles on the radio, they sounded jarring. They didn't really feel at home. They sounded fine in discos, but radio . . . So, when I heard 'Promised You A Miracle' on the radio, I burst out grinning!"* JIM

" *If you had asked me last year what somebody who wrote a hit single was like, I'd definitely have said they have weird ears."* JIM

" *If we had to write a hit single consciously, we really would have missed the mark. Some people, like the guys in B.E.F. (The British Electric Foundation, the core of which became Heaven 17) for example, understand structure and know what the man in the street wants to hear. They know the right word for the right chord. They know that if you only had two more DBs on that snare you'd have sold 20,000 more in Finland or something. They're students of pop, but we've never really studied it."* JIM

" *This is the crazy Catch 22. I can see people thinking this is more contrived than anything we've done before, but I think the things we did before were actually more contrived. Our music has always been honest about showing its influences, but I think the influences we used to use, or portray, were the darker ones. I mean, I don't get up in the morning and play Robert Fripp or Nico records, more likely Diana Ross or Chic. We'd never really showed that though, because I think we wanted to be taken more seriously."* JIM

" *I seem to be fitting in perfectly. The day I stepped into the studio I found Simple Minds had a completely different approach to music. They changed my whole attitude."* MEL

" *I love power, you know. I love powerful music. I love powerful images and things . . . But, what I'm absolutely charmed by, is quiet power."* JIM

" *We've got a better bass and drum section now than any funk band in Britain, and a guitarist and keyboard player who could play on Genesis or Roxy Music albums."* JIM

" *I like to keep in touch with my family, because this whole thing could stop next year – you never know – and it's nice to know I could go back home. I phone them a lot, and they let me know what's going on. My mother works in a sweet shop, and all the schoolkids come in and tell her what they think of the new record. My dad works on building sites. Most of the band did that too, at the start, just to get money to buy equipment. We've always had an Art School tag which, although I didn't mind, I did always think was really funny. I don't even think there is an art school in Glasgow. And if there is, they certainly wouldn't have us."* JIM

" *It's time for a dark horse to come through. There's Human League, Soft Cell, Haircut 100 . . . well, we can be as bouncy and boyish as any of them, but we've also got an undercurrent that we're proud of. There hasn't been a young*

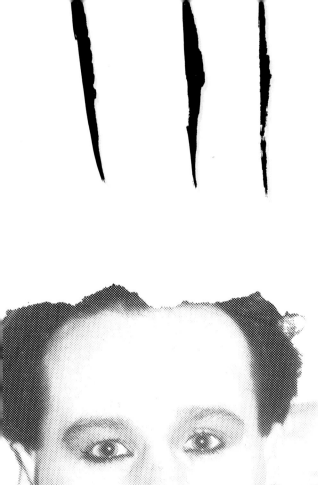

band with an undercurrent since, well, The Doors. Now, they could be AOR, they had different sides. The Velvet Underground as well. Loads of other bands were influenced by different sides of those bands. You don't get that nowadays, but I think we could be the ones, we could win through." JIM

"This is a real transitional period for us. I've been writing a lot as always, but it's not so much names and places now. It would be a joke to take that further. The story begins with 'I Travel' and finishes with 'Seeing Out The Angel'. I wouldn't want to be the travel correspondent of Western music, or for people to know what to expect from a Simple Minds album." JIM

"When I saw U2 on television recently, I saw the same look in their eyes when they were playing, as I've seen in ours in our live videos. We both look transfixed and yet transported, as if we'd seen a vision. All the recent pictures I've seen of myself, I'm standing with my arms open – whereas I always used to be fists clenched, arms crossed, holding myself in." JIM

"At the same time as we were out in Australia, Echo And The Bunnymen were out there, like a lot of British bands who are where we are at the moment, many of us are from the same background. I watched them being interviewed on TV – and I love them as a band – and they were really bored. How rock people 'should' be, you could just see. With us though . . . we go to play first, and find that with our eyes and our ears open, a chance to talk to people, young people, we all seem to come back with a lot of ideas." JIM

"We're not playing more than 10 dates in Britain, because it was horrible on our last tour. People would come to the soundcheck with our albums for us to sign, and we'd have a chat with them and say, 'See you at the gig tonight then.' And they'd reply, 'Nope, we can't afford it.' I know there's a depression, but it's much more evident in the UK than anywhere else. It's so gloomy. After the gig there's nothing to do apart from go back to your hotel room. But I love touring abroad . . . because you're so far removed from reality. You can fall in love with someone every 15 minutes." JIM

"I'm always being asked why we're bothering to play daft places like Sweden and Australia. It's because we sell four times as many records out there!" JIM

"There's a point that most bands reach on tour, when they feel like they're really regressing – it's beginning to damage them mentally in some way. But I think if you can have something that's well put together – so well that you can actually see the progress – then it's the greatest thing in the world. Every bit as inspiring as sitting down for four weeks and writing an album, for me anyway." CHARLIE

"I love hotel living. You can be any kind of eccentric millionaire. I usually say I'm an architect, because they never believe me when I say I'm a pop singer. They've never seen me on TV." JIM

"There's a sort of prejudice in Britain just now, these leftist stringers, the angry brigade who keep calling us capitalists . . . The great thing about us, is that the spirit's so big that it could never be broken by anything like that." JIM

" *I hate all the new trendy bands – all that teenage rebel stuff – they make their audience feel inferior because they haven't got the right haircut.* " JIM

" *People often try too hard. I feel sorry for people sometimes because, in a strong attempt to be innovative, they actually become so contrived that it's got no value whatsoever. They'd have been better doing the most natural thing, even if it was as clichéd as anything. It would still have a bit more integrity, and people would see it. The important thing isn't that you have to justify not sounding like the past. Nowadays people are more or less saying, 'The reason we use these chords is because we don't want to sound like something in the past.' It's not, 'This is the way we want to sound,' it's 'We don't want to sound like that.' "* CHARLIE

"I saw Killing Joke on Top Of The Pops, and they weren't threatening at all. It's not a question of dressing in leather and studs. It's a look in the eye." JIM

"I've always hated the idea of ignorance, because it always seemed to me like some kind of slavery. It always appealed to me to be able to have an understanding of a wide range of subjects." JIM

"Our LPs have been projects in a way, and this one ('New Gold Dream') felt like us putting together songs which had already been verified as classics." CHARLIE

"I like the image of the cross on the album sleeve ('New Gold dream'). It pleases me. I used to wear a Communist hammer and sickle, but not because I'm a Communist or anything. I simply like the shape." JIM

"People ask me if I've been born again, and I say no. I didn't have to be born again. I've never been away." JIM

"I reckon that in two years time, if we keep up the same rate, people looking back on our albums will be talking about two different bands – Simple Minds pre 'New Gold Dream', and simple Minds after. We're not trying to be smug, but we know that we have to top it next year. We seem to have a weird competitiveness with ourselves, and 'New Gold Dream' has set a standard. It's definitely in step with the films that have come out this year, and the politics of this year. 'King Is White And In The Crowd' was inspired when I saw the Sadat killing – it's a song about an assassin. Without trying to be trendy with it, the threads of events and happenings are always there, but under the surface. I'd love this band to be a diary." JIM

"**W**e're nowhere near as technical as we often get credited for. All the rhythm patterns come from playing about. When something happens we just tape it, and it becomes the seeds of a song." JIM

"**P**eter Walsh is a really good producer. We put so much in, and he takes it out again. But the effect isn't less, it's more." JIM

"**W**hen we finished 'New Gold Dream', I remember phoning up Bruce, our manager, and saying, 'We've really kinda surpassed what we should be.' And he's going, 'It's two o'clock in the morning, what are you rabbiting on about?' And I was just going, 'You don't understand!' Those backing tracks were just so enormous, I was just really afraid of trying to find a voice and a sentiment that could match them. Inside I knew that I had them, but it was just a matter of bringing it out without going over that fine line that divides grandeur from pomposity. Eventually I had one day left, and I was just forced to do it. I had all these pages with phrases on them, and I just formed the structure of the songs as I went along. Then, when I came out and I knew it had worked, it was just a brilliant feeling, but a feeling of danger that you'd attained something that you'd got no right to . . . you'd reached a point you really shouldn't have reached." JIM

"**S**ometimes I'm not too sure what a lot of our songs are about. I'm not sure what I'm searching for. Is it a theory? Is it a person? Is it a God? Is it a new pair of shoes?" JIM

"**P**eter (Walsh) never made the band go in a way we didn't want to, but he picked up one side of us as opposed to a kind of overallness. When you hear 'New Gold Dream' live, the tracks go whoosh! As for the album, I dunno. There's a lot of good things been said about it, and I like that. But other people say it's ethereal mush, and that doesn't upset me either." JIM

"**I** was really pleased that we managed to break through and hadn't lost ourselves. We hadn't brought on any star producer who had an arm-load of hits behind him, because we felt that we'd come so far and then put it into the lap of someone else." JIM

"**I** used to need the egotism of being credited as the lyricist . . . I used to feel insecure because I didn't play any instrument. But now I'm totally satisfied with being part of a five-piece band." JIM

"**I** go through periods of being a real pig. I could just get into the hotel, do the soundcheck, check out what the girls are like, sort of thing. But I just end up feeling disgusted. I really do." JIM

"**I** think about the band all the time. So when it comes to an opinion being asked, I've always got an answer, and I get it out first." JIM

"**N**ew Gold Dream' is a coffee table album . . . a nice thing to have in your home. But I don't think there have been many albums where you've got the coffee table on the surface, but there are worms in the wood underneath. Our next album will be one of the worms." JIM

january

Simple Minds shut themselves away in a Lincolnshire retreat, where they try to compose new material.

february

Derek Forbes writes a children's book, *The Adventures Of Sally And The Moon People.*

march

Back in Europe, the band have a good time in Italy, but are disappointed by poor ticket sales in Germany. Scandinavia fares better however, and proves a good warm-up for America and Canada.

april

Simple Minds go down a storm in Los Angeles and San Francisco, but face a cooler reception in the southern States. In New York the show goes well, but Jim comes to grief when he's attacked outside his hotel by the jealous boyfriend of a committed female fan. Seems the girl in question had visited Kerr's room the day before, and her fella had just found out about it. Jim suffers a broken nose, while his assailant goes away with broken ribs and two black eyes for his trouble.

may

Quite apart from Kerr's battle scars, the band realise they've *all* been pushing their luck too far. Mick is now complaining of a stress-related stomach complaint, and even Charlie is beginning to suffer the rigours of life on the road. They decide to take a break while they can. Jim and Charlie set off for a cycling holiday in India, while Mick, Mel and Derek head for the more traditional sun spots of the Mediterranean.

june

Now fully rejuvenated, Simple Minds go back on the road and play a series of open air events right across Europe.

july

While appearing at the Turnhout-Werchter festival in Belgium, Simple Minds meet up with U2 for the first time. They get along so well that Bono and Jim Kerr embark on an impromptu duet.

The band return to Nomis Studios, London, where they record some more demos.

august

As a result of the Belgian meeting, Simple Minds are invited to appear as 'special guests' at U2's all day event at Phoenix Park, Dublin. Eurythmics and Big Country also share the bill. Jim sings 'Waterfront' for the first time.

september

The month is spent rehearsing new songs at Rockfield Studios.

october

The constant stream of rehearsals, demos and more rehearsals comes to an end, and Simple Minds finally enter the Virgin Townhouse Studios in Shepherds Bush to record the follow-up to 'New Gold Dream'. Steve Lillywhite is producing, much to the delight of Jim and Charlie, who are particularly impressed by his work with Peter Gabriel and U2. Naming the album 'Sparkle In The Rain', the group decide to keep it under wraps until the New Year.

november

Simple Minds release 'Waterfront', their first single in 12 months. They also play a free one-off date at the Barrowland Ballroom, in Glasgow, and film the event for a

ON the waterfront.

promotional video of the single. The venue is reopened especially for the occasion and, henceforth, once again becomes a major link in the North's fast-developing rock circuit. Failing to reach the Top 10, 'Waterfront' drops short at 13.

december

The band celebrate a successful year, with a short burst of pre-Christmas shows in London and Glasgow. Not surprisingly, Barrowland is booked for the Scottish shows.

" *You have to be a bit of a fruitcake to do interviews and analyse the thing that you didn't analyse in the first place.*" JIM

" *The whole pop thing is so confused, everybody's got their heads up their arses.*" JIM

" *It's hard to know where your destination lies, because we never planned anything from the start. We can't really remember saying 'Let's make a band', and if you ask any of us what our ambition is, I don't think anybody would really know.*" JIM

" *The American trip was a highlight for me, especially when I got to meet Herbie Hancock. I went round to his house and his wee 13-year-old daughter opened the door – she'd been to see us the night before – and all her schoolfriends were round there wanting autographs. My autograph. So here's*

me standing right next to one of my all-time heroes, signing autographs!"
MICK

" I *met Stevie Wonder in Hollywood. He said he'd played 'Promised You
A Miracle' 40 times on the run. He was right into us."* DEREK

" T*here was a crazy period at the end of the seventies when it was
embarrassing, apparently, just to be in a band that made records and
toured. All sorts of terms came up, from 'rockist', to people forming their own
little limited companies. Touring was out, and playing was out. There seemed
to be so much talk. We've always wanted to be as modern as tomorrow but, in
doing that, we're one of the most traditional bands out, in as much as we play
and make records . . . Some people think we should take a stance against the
routine of recording an album, and then going through the whole process of
touring for eight months. But I don't know what else we could desire."* JIM

" M*ost bands are not playing live, because they just fucking can't. I still
think there's nothing better than if you get a brilliant band in a big hall
with a lot of people."* JIM

" W*e did find things getting a bit safe on tour though, that's why we started
playing Lou Reed's 'Street Hassle'. Up till then we were playing the
same set every night – almost playing it with our eyes shut, and still going
down great. So we said, 'Let's put it back on the edge, let's do a song we don't
really know.' I mean, I don't actually know the full words, and there's no
arrangement to it either. It's great to come to a show and, right at the last
minute, just put your head on the chopping block."* JIM

" The European dates brought us back to a kinda raw stage, I think. Some nights it was really rough, and a couple of the crew were slagging us off . . . but they also knew we were creating a real good feeling." JIM

" I think we probably were overdoing things a bit, that's why we had a holiday. Jim and I just had the most amazing experience in India. We went to Katmandu and the Taj Mahal. We even had this wild idea of climbing the Himalayas, but we decided against it in the end. The people were incredible though. They had an amazing beauty, and although they were living in abject poverty, they just seemed so happy." CHARLIE

" I'd really like to do something great. I don't think we've done anything great yet. We used to believe we were going to be a small band, we'd maybe acquire a bit of hipness or something, but now I can see us becoming much more of a force." JIM

" When we started this tour (promoting 'New Gold Dream), at the first soundcheck I heard the sound and knew the show was going to be absolutely brilliant. It looked great on stage with the lights and everything. I knew we were going to play well, and the support band were China Crisis, and all for three quid, or three-fifty. All that's got to do with why it's selling out." JIM

" We are without doubt one of the best bands in Britain right now, if not the world. In the old days we used to keep praising our influences. We don't need to do that now. We don't feel beneath anybody." JIM

" *We* suddenly feel confident about doing all kinds of things now – like colour photo sessions – because we now recognise the need for them. It's the same with letters from fans. I see the need for that too. No matter who they're from, young or old, they all want a piece of your heart ultimately. Before, it all seemed like a throwback from the past, like the girls running after The Beatles . . . But now, I'd much rather have an attractive girl sitting listening to our music, than get on the front page of a music paper." JIM

" *I'd* like to be a little more settled. Apparently, I'm unbearable to live with when we stop touring. So I think I'll have to stop some of my nonsense in that way. The thing about me, is that I'm terribly selfish." JIM

" *When* we came back off the road, we sat down and wrote these new songs, feeling very chuffed and smug. But a week later we found out all we were doing was writing 'New Gold Dream' Part Two, which was really awful. It was a big problem at the beginning of the year (1983). I was drying up. Everything I wrote seemed to be either the same as 'New Gold Dream' or a parody of it. Which is why there hasn't been an album all year, because this mental block came on." JIM

" *To* break the block I went back to Glasgow . . . I went for a walk one night and ended up literally on the banks of the Clyde. I went right to where the town ends, to what were once the shipyards. It was eerie. All I could hear were my own footsteps, and I was surrounded by factories that are just shells now. I just started to think what it was like in its day. Some of my people, my grandfather and stuff, had worked there. There was a predominant bleakness, but the great thing was being able to see the water. It was still moving and seemed to hold some kind of symbol, because it was there when the city was first built, and it'll still be there when the city goes. It's not being romantic but . . . I still believe things will turn round and life will go back there and strength will still come from there. It just made me write a few simple words, just a verse, an anecdote even, which happened to fit a backing track that came up. There was no European in it, no President getting shot, no fugitives, but it was important for me and for anyone listening to the song . . . 'Waterfront'." JIM

" *I* don't attach too much importance to the words . . . If they sound attractive and make a coherent picture, then great." JIM

" *This* time round ('Sparkle In The Rain') we hadn't meant to work with Steve Lillywhite at all . . . we'd actually wanted to use Alex Sadkin. We liked the stuff he'd done with Bob Marley and Grace Jones. You could see his face light up when he heard us play. He agreed to do it, but then he went off and did Duran Duran, Classix Nouveaux and The Thompson Twins, and we thought – 'What's going on here?' It just fell apart." JIM

" *Steve* Lillywhite brought out all the energy we normally reserve for interviews or concerts, and we knew beforehand if anybody was able to do that, it was him. You can actually hear Charlie's guitar on this record and . . . you can even hear the words on a few tracks. On 'Waterfront', I remember when Derek came in with the bass line, it could've been Status Quo." JIM

" *Barrowland* was notorious in the sixties. It was the home ground for all the gang violence of the period." CHARLIE

january

Simple Minds appear on TV's *Oxford Roadshow*, alongside label-mates China Crisis. Another new single, 'Speed Your Love To Me', hits the airwaves. Meanwhile, to escape winter, the group fly to Australia and New Zealand, where they play a series of festivals with the likes of Eurythmics, Talking Heads and – cue fanfare – The Pretenders. Jim meets Chrissie Hynde for the first time, and falls in love.

february

By the end of the month 'Sparkle In The Rain' is released, and goes straight into the album chart at number one. 'Speed Your Love to Me' peaks at 20. They also embark on a massive UK tour, with dates at Galway, Cork, Dublin, Belfast, Edinburgh, Dundee, Aberdeen and Glasgow.

march

The trek continues with shows at Newcastle, Liverpool, Nottingham, Manchester, Leeds, Brighton, Southampton, Bristol, Leicester and Birmingham. This is as far as they get for the time being however, since a rather nasty flu virus gets the better of Jim, and several further dates have to be postponed.
'Up On The Catwalk' is released. A third single from 'Sparkle In The Rain', it just scrapes into the Top 30.

april

Now fully recovered, Jim dashes to Europe where he joins the rest of his band for a major European tour.

may

Jim disappears to New York where he marries Chrissie Hynde at a secret ceremony in the city's notorious Central Park. Doing the deed in style, they exchange vows in the back of a horse-drawn carriage.
Back in Britain, Simple Minds fulfil their commitment with a series of dates held over from earlier in the year. Shows at Cornwall and Poole are added, while seven nights at London's Hammersmith Odeon have now become eight – thus equalling Elton John's 1982 record.

june

Exhausted, the band take a short break.

july

Simple Minds support The Pretenders on a lengthy Stateside jaunt. Things don't go *badly*, but they're still finding America the toughest nut to crack.

october

The band book into a rehearsal studio — Barwell Court, in Surrey — which is owned by Derek Forbes' idol, a session bassist called John Giblin. They're trying to write material which could help them in their quest to conquer the States, but keep being interrupted by record company demands to meet with songwriter and producer, Keith Forsey. Perhaps best known for his work with Billy Joel, Forsey has a track which is scheduled to appear in a new American movie, *The Breakfast Club*. Bryan Ferry has already turned it down, and he's hoping Simple Minds will record it instead.

november

Submitting to record company pressure, Simple Minds record Forsey's number, 'Don't You (Forget About Me)', during a three-hour stint in a crummy north London studio. They leave as quickly as they can, and promptly forget all about the song, which they never expect to hear much of again.

december

Simple Minds play three Christmas gigs at Barrowland, which are sold out long before they're publicised in the music press. There's talk of recording the shows for immediate release as a live album, though plans of this nature are postponed for the time being.

"*Sparkle In The Rain' is just manic. I don't know how we went from 'New Gold Dream' to that, but we did. One track, 'Kick Inside Of Me' sounded like a Sex Pistols track.*" JIM

"*My fingers were physically bleeding from playing 'Kick Inside Of Me'. I just went mad.*" DEREK

"*Our rock is dead hard. It hasn't got rock clichés, but rock dynamism. We're going for the giant sound . . .*" JIM

"*The criticisms of 'Sparkle In The Rain' are just . . . crap. We could have written those reviews, in fact, we did write them. We're dead in control now, and I think that shines through. Review wise, for us there are certain people who dismissed us this time last year, and who now go out of their way to say we're crap – and will use four or five paragraphs to do it!*" JIM

"*The worst kind of disease in Britain and Europe right now is apathy. Apathy creeps up and locks itself around people, and then it's really hard to get rid of. I don't think the bomb's going to go off. If I did, I'd just stay in bed all day – it'd be hypocritical to do what we're doing right now. I'm naïve enough to say that good can be more powerful than evil. I'll put my head on the line and say that darkness doesn't have to win.*" JIM

"*It's a challenge to sell a million records or more, and to do it with dignity, style and grace – to do it with music that doesn't patronise, doesn't condescend, doesn't tranquillise.*" JIM

"*Glamour isn't worth anything. It's a fairytale world which has nothing to do with life at all. I certainly don't call myself a 'rock star'. I wouldn't lower myself to that label.*" JIM

"*I've got a sense of pride and discipline, so I'd never take a stream of pretty women to bed with me. I want to smash a lot of the dreadful image that surrounds rock and pop.*" JIM

"*Everything relies on money, and it's difficult for decent bands to break through. You're expected to arrive in a blaze of glory, and work your way down from there.*" JIM

JIM and Chrissie: ascloseasthis.

PROMOTIONAL shots from the 'Up On The Catwalk' video.

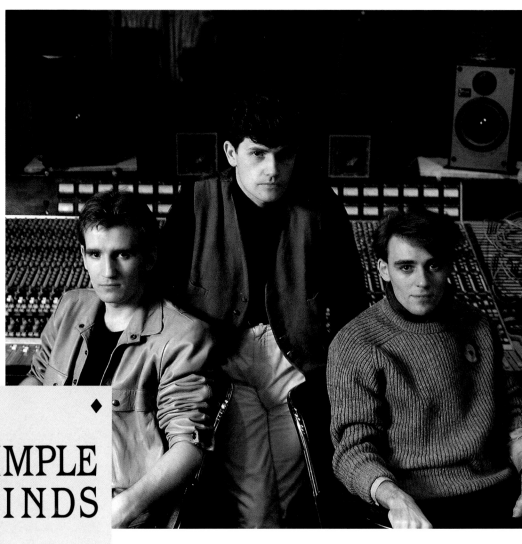

SIMPLE MINDS

TOUR brochure for 'Sparkle In The Rain'.

" *If Graham Greene can write a fantastic book at 65, why shouldn't John Lennon have written a great song at 60? The whole idea of the generation gap has to be smashed in rock. Ever since Eddie Cochran and 'Summertime Blues' it's been the same. You're still getting groups like Wham!, doing things like 'Bad Boys', and saying that when you're 16 you've got to rebel against your parents. That's terrible, that's discrimination. I think you learn from your parents, and they learn from you. Let's face it, the generation gap must get smaller. If I have children, there won't be many things they'll be able to do that will surprise me. It's those clichés that have to be smashed.* " JIM

" *I think a lot of the things I said in interviews last year have annoyed people – just the tone of it. But I think there's a certain glow in my interviews. They're usually picturesque and pretty entertaining, which is more than can be said for the Paul Wellers of this world.* " JIM

" *I didn't think I'd get married, but I really believe in the family. I like the idea of a woman and a man who stay together – and who live together – but looking around I felt that it doesn't actually work. What can I say? For me it felt right. I'm aware of the pros and cons of it. I'm also new to it, very new to it. I think it's a question which could be better answered in 10 years' time. Or having had 10 years' problems solved.* " JIM

" **C**hrissie's group (The Pretenders) have much more of a rock audience than we do. We did all these gigs with them in the Midwest, where kids would come out with their popcorn and their Pepsi. They'd just look at our clothes and think, 'No, not our kind of band . . .'" JIM

" **W**e do go mad when a record comes out, running around and talking. At the end of 1982, I looked at myself and thought I looked like I should be in a band. I'd always denied the danger of being on tour for a year. I always said it would never catch up with us because we had too much energy. But last year when we got back, in one week we got just about everything that means 'thumbs up' from the music industry – be it gold discs, or front pages, or topping a lot of the polls. I'm not saying we're ungrateful bastards, but we never felt up or down. I think it was due to total fatigue and being generally knackered. And that's a bit frightening." JIM

" **W**hen we play live, something comes over me. I feel much bigger than I am. I feel less clumsy, more agile and less vulnerable. I look to see who's around me and I feel very very strong." JIM

january

Simple Minds decide on a breather.

march

The Breakfast Club becomes an immediate box office success. Its theme song, 'Don't You (Forget About Me)', goes straight to the top of the US charts. No one is more surprised than Simple Minds, who still refuse to include the track on their forthcoming album.

Jim becomes a father, when Chrissie Hynde gives birth to a bouncing baby girl. The couple name her Jasmine Paris. It's Chrissie's second child — she already has a young daughter, Natalie Rae, by Kinks boss Ray Davies.

april

Longstanding bassist Derek Forbes quits the group in what is *publicly* described as a 'purely amicable split'. However, it's generally considered that a rift has been developing for some time, and rumours around the music business suggest Forbes has been sacked for his slackening commitment to the band. Said to be keen to pursue a solo career however, the bass player will later turn up in the ranks of ZTT's Propaganda where, coincidentally, he will again join forces with Brian McGee.

Forbes' replacement turns out to be a session player, famed for his contributions to work by Peter Gabriel, Phil Collins and Kate Bush. He's also the owner of a well-used rehearsal studio in Surrey. Yes, it's none other than John Giblin . . .

may

The band continue to develop ideas for the next album. With Kerr now a father, the lyrics begin to follow a more directly political path, as parental responsibilities begin to weigh heavily on the singer's shoulders.

Simple Minds finally start recording their eighth LP, at Virgin's Townhouse Studios, with plans to mix the material in New York. Switching producers yet again, the band are now working with the popular American pairing of Jimmy Iovine and Bob Clearmountain who, between them, have twiddled knobs for the likes of John Lennon, U2, Tom Petty, The Stones, Chic, The Pretenders, David Bowie and Bruce Springsteen. The credentials are there all right and Jimmy, especially, proves an invaluable aid at the composition stage — helping the group tighten up the creative process, and generally encouraging them towards a bigger, more panoramic style of music. The band also call in session singer Robyn Clark. Kerr always liked her voice on Bowie's 'Young Americans' album, and is looking for a similar contribution.

july

Midway through preparations for their new album, Simple Minds play the Philadelphia leg of *Live Aid*. Like so many other artists who appeared in either London or Philadelphia, their career is given a terrific boost through the event, and their short set – which includes the American hit 'Don't You (Forget About Me)' – finally establishes them in America.

september

A new single, 'Alive And Kicking', is released, and represents their first *original* material since March 1984. The accompanying video is shot in New York, by Poland's Oscar winning director Zbigniew Rybcznski. And why not . . .?

october

The new album, 'Once Upon A Time' is finally unveiled. A long time coming, it's well received by the record buying public, with two million copies being sold during the first two months of its shelf-life. Its release also heralds the start of a 15-month world tour, an excursion that will go a long way to promote not only the album, but also the group's favourite political cause – Amnesty International.

november

Back in Canada and the States, Simple Minds really start to capitalise on their new-found fame and popularity, and begin to make the move from 'arenas' to 'stadiums'. At every show, The Minds take full opportunity to explain the work of Amnesty – an organisation busily campaigning on behalf of all 'prisoners of conscience'.

december

The group launch their biggest European tour to date, visiting Holland, France and Belgium before Christmas.

" *A lot of people said these were great achievements, that the band had scaled new heights, but we were so jaded we didn't feel any real excitement at all. We could have played a set with our eyes closed. We were our own worst enemies in that we'd never take a break. This time we had to.* " JIM

" *There is a war on within us now. Simple Minds music has to get across. There is a need. You look out now and there's so much music that's just dead wood. We have to try and show that there's a side to this rock game other than just hamburger music. And if that means beating them at their own game, then we must beat them at their own game.* " JIM

" *Don't You (Forget About Me)' . . . that's the irony in the Simple Minds tale. You pressure your bollocks off for years, then you do something effortlessly in an instant, and it turns out to be the key . . . It was really quite a* "

twist of fate, opened all these doors for us. We were in a spot and just decided
that this was the best thing to do. What were we gonna say? 'No, we're The
Minds, we don't do that kind of thing,' ha!" JIM

"We always wanted to do music for films. Mick and Charlie write tons
of atmospheric stuff that would be great for soundtracks. 'Don't You
(Forget About Me)' isn't exactly an atmospheric song, it's more like the type of
song we were doing two or three years ago. But it was offered to us during our
break when we weren't feeling very precious about our art . . . We don't want
people to think this is the new direction we're going in though. It's nothing like
the ideas we have in our heads. It was just something nice to do that, hopefully,
will get us known in the film world." JIM

"Simple Minds have always had these trying periods. It was something we
really had to think about. When Brian left, it didn't really pose as much of
a problem as when Derek left. Derek came up with some great bass lines, and
he had a lot of fans. So the balance and the musical chemistry changes. Like,
normally we would write a song and we would start with the bass line. This
album, we didn't start with any bass lines. We sort of worked in reverse, but
that wasn't any problem. It was more just a new way of doing things, another
challenge." CHARLIE

"Two years ago we played in Montreal to 60 or 70 people, this time we played
an ice hockey arena! And then I read a review of the show and it really

JIM calls the tune and the line-up changes. Above left: John Giblin replaces Derek Forbes.

slammed us. It was all this 'Simple Minds have gone big time and are playing stadium rock' . . . and all these other derogatory terms. The fact is, it's a challenge to play anywhere, from the smallest club to the biggest stadium, and I think we can handle it. I saw The Jam play in a club and they were fantastic, and I saw them play a stadium and they were awful. Their music doesn't have the size or the scope to fit in these halls. Our music is suited to these halls, and it's where we'll probably be for the next period. I've seen bands in these halls and it doesn't always work, but then you can go and see someone like Peter Gabriel, who brings you to the music, and you forget you're in an auditorium. You feel you're in a much smaller place. And if the band can do that, then it's a good thing. In our case, to deny the music that, and to deny the people that, would be wrong. If 12,000 people want to see us, we'll play a 12,000 seater. If 200 people want to see us, then we'll play somewhere smaller. We can handle it." JIM

*"*W*ith 'Once Upon A Time', it was certainly the right moment to come up front and drop every idea that we might have been hiding behind. Jimmy Iovine played dumber than dumb. I would write something that, to me, would be as plain as day, and he would go, 'What's that? That could be a million things. What's it mean to me? I don't want to have to think to your records!' He did what I wanted someone to do. He took the pseud out of me."* JIM

*"*I *think I've always been conscious of being part of a family, and perhaps I'm a bit more conscious of it now. But to me it's all one family, the family I came from, and the family I'm now in . . . I guess it has affected me. I was reading an interview in an American magazine, it was two or three-years-old, and it was with the wife of the Polish Solidarity leader, Lech Walesa, at the time when he had been taken into captivity. And reading it made me think about women in general, the wives of the miners as well . . . I began to think what it would be like for me if, for some reason, I couldn't see my daughter. And I would never have thought about that this time last year. It inspired me to write 'All The Things She Said'."* JIM

SIMPLE Minds in the Live Aid photo booth, Philadelphia 1985.

*"*I*t felt great playing Live Aid, it really did. Although, on the day, things moved so fast that . . . even now it's hard to recollect any memories or anything. I was just really chuffed that I got Jack Nicholson's autograph! I met him about 20 minutes before I went on stage and that's what was going through my mind a lot of the time we were playing. The rest was just a haze. On the outside you could imagine what the backstage area was like, and a few people have said to me it must have been terrible with all those egos – but it wasn't like that. At night, when Duran Duran and Mick Jagger came, suddenly you needed three or four passes to get places – instead of one pass in the day – but it was great. In fact, my heart went out to Madonna. She was just about to get married and she turned up backstage with Sean Penn, and everyone was just like a swarm of flies around her. At the time she was probably the biggest star in the world, yet she was just sitting there putting on her mascara like there was no big deal. It was really good."* JIM

*"*G*lasgow's in my blood. People in Glasgow are great, because they tend to call a spade a spade. But it's a bit hard when you're walking down the street and someone says, 'Hey, I heard your new album – thought it was a load of crap!'"* JIM

february

After extensive touring round Germany, Scandinavia, Switzerland and Italy, Simple Minds at last return to the UK, and face inevitable flack from the hardline music press. More successful than ever, the band are deemed to have earned intolerable recognition from the masses and so, not surprisingly, can no longer be revered by serious-minded journalists.

One wilting dufflecoat after another writes off the group's flourishing success and yet, somewhat curiously, hoards of hacks *still* ask to be included on guest lists for the current batch of shows in Birmingham, Glasgow and London. Sad but true, a few fans fall for the oldest gag in music journalism, and allow themselves to be put off. Oh yes, and 'Sanctify Yourself' is released as a single.

Simple Minds recent show at Rotterdam's Ahoy Stadium is televised by *The Tube*.

march

All profits from their Wembley Arena show are donated to Amnesty International. 'All The Things She Said' becomes the third single to be unleashed from 'Once Upon A Time'.

april

Jim reportedly buys a new house just outside Edinburgh, a property which is said to have once been owned by Robert Louis Stevenson.

Simple Minds begin a 44-date tour of the US. Starting in the deep south, the band work their way between the east and west coasts over the next couple of months — finally ending up in Canada.

june

Headlining a string of summer festivals in Europe, Simple Minds are *nowhere* more successful than when they play their own back yard — Glasgow's Ibrox Stadium. However, their performance at a couple of shows in Milton Keynes *does* come a very close second.

Interestingly, when they play Dublin's Croke Park, the group are joined on stage by former bassist Derek Forbes, much to the delight of the sell-out crowd.

august

Jim and the boys bring their European shows to a close at The Zenyth in Paris, where two consecutive nights are recorded for a prospective live album — to be released next year.

september

A world tour, which has seen Simple Minds play to around two million people, at last enters its final phase — a trip to Australia, New Zealand and Japan.

november

The group release a new single, 'Ghostdancing', and duly donate all proceeds from the song to Amnesty International. For a band who'd seemed to have kept their political beliefs private for so long, they now look relieved to be jumping off the fence.

TOP: 'Once Upon A Time' tour brochure. Above and right: In and around Essen, Germany.

" *There are no cult bands any more . . . they're either commercial failures, or commercial successes.*" JIM

" *I talk to fans a lot and there are people who say, 'Well, you're not really our band any more.' And I understand that. Because when you're young you carve out your own identity with the bands that are the soundtrack to your years. And there're always those people who go for that thing of being sort of obscure. They don't take what is strong on the radio . . . and it's more personal*

'cos they're the only guy in school with 'Raw Power', or something like that. I can tolerate that from 15, 16, 17-year-olds, but one thing I hate, and always have hated, is élitism. And this thing that 'They're my band' is like saying it's membership to some club with an on-the-door policy!" JIM

" *A cult following is the greatest thing to have as a grass roots foundation, but it can also be a real pain in the arse. The fans sometimes just want to tie your wrists. Look what Dylan got when he went electric! Think of that!! It's really really immature. Piss off! If Dylan wants to do something different, fine. If we want to go on stage with trumpets, then that's fine too. We accept the consequences – as I'm sure Bob Dylan does as well.*" JIM

" *I feel sorry for people who were conned by punk. I saw through it early on. People really believed it was a revolution, but it was more like a few art students flippin' the bird to the establishment. No one's ever felt threatened by a dodgy haircut! It was really hokey. The language was all 'anarchy' and 'riot'. I don't know, I'll always be attracted to things with beauty in them . . .*

And that's probably why so many critics now think of us as being the new musical outcasts – the rock dinosaurs of our generation . . . I can't deny that I've thought about it myself. It is something that's crossed my mind. Yeah, we've talked about it. Not so much as the band, but I've talked to Bono about that. Like the way 'stadium' is just spoken with disdain, for instance, especially with reference to the seventies bands that played them. But don't forget that we've had the chance to look at some of the mistakes that those bands made. Not in terms of the music even, but just the way it was then, with this cocoon of people around you, the way that rock people were meant to act – TVs out the windows, limousines, that whole circus. I don't think that exists at all with us. We just go out and play, and every year the crowds get bigger. Besides which, it's not where you play, it's how you play." JIM

" *O*ld bands may have killed stadium rock, but recent bands are bringing it to life again. It's like these artists who say that home taping is killing music. Duff music is killing music! It's as simple as that. Home taping encourages music, so does bootlegging. Enthusiasm encourages. So bands went into stadiums and just didn't know how to do it – they were going on stoned out of their minds, being led on. Why should we feel at all responsible for the stupidity of people 10 years ago? Why should we ever feel part of the stigma?!" JIM

" *I*t was incredible playing Ibrox. I just stood there and savoured the atmosphere. I was drunk on the whole atmosphere of the place. It's a treasure." JIM

" *I* never think the people come to see me. I think the music has a magnet, and we really do detach the music from ourselves. I think that's the difference between our band and a lot of bands. We're still trying to work out where our music comes from and, when you try and do that, especially in an interview situation, you end up coming out with adjectives that make you look mystical or mysterious." JIM

" *T*here's something inside the music that comforts. It's very important when you get a letter from somebody that says, 'I was feeling very lonely, very desperate, and I heard your record on the radio and I feel much better.'" JIM

" *I*n America we get a lot of knickers thrown on stage. It's kind of weird. I just wonder how they get them off." JIM

" *I*t was brilliant to see Springsteen become the biggest superstar in the world last year, regardless of what anyone thinks about his music. You know that if he's not 100 per cent there then he's 99 per cent there. Whereas all these other megastars have gone totally whacko, like Michael Jackson and Prince . . . It's also amazing how susceptible people are to the guy who's made an act out of being the man of the people – Billy Bragg – the way he was portrayed as being totally there when two years earlier he was driving a fucking tank. But none of the smart journalists mentioned that. How can you trust a guy like that?" JIM

" *T*he music business in America is very corrupt. It's very easy to be bought in there, but whether you stick around or not is something else." JIM

"**C**ompromise is when you do something that you would rather not do, but you do it for some diplomatic reason. That didn't go on. We obviously wanted to be on the radio. It wasn't a compromise, we wanted to be on it." JIM

"**I**n the past couple of years we've come to appreciate the power that money brings. It gives you the ability to decide not to do the Terry Wogan show, not to do the Noel Edmunds show, not to do Top Of The Pops. You can make those kind of decisions independent of financial pressures." JIM

"**W**e've made a lot of money this year, but it's the first time we've made money in eight years together. So, in comparison with someone who's worked on the oil rigs for eight years, I don't know if we're rich or not. I've got mates who went to Saudi Arabia to work, and they're richer than me." JIM

"**S**uccess brings media space. It costs absolutely nothing, and it's a waste if we don't use it. You get your space, and you've got the chance to say 'Pepsi Cola' or 'Amnesty International'. You don't get paid for plugging Amnesty, but at least you get to sleep at night." JIM

"**P**ublicly supporting Amnesty International . . . was, in a sense, a safe issue for me – because I didn't feel out of my depth. Also because I think, in a traditional sense, it's a very rock 'n' roll cause in terms of freedom of speech, freedom of thought." JIM

"**W**e really do make twats of ourselves when we talk about what we do. because we always seem to rise to the bait." JIM

"**I** don't think any of the books have got it right in relation to sexuality. I don't think any of the religions have got it right. The celibacy thing is asking for trouble." JIM

"**I** think of my marriage the same way as I think of my parents' marriage. This life is like a gold mountain. You've got to keep one foot on it, and the rest of you off." JIM

"**I** think Chrissie (Hynde) is an original. I'll go and buy four Bob Dylan tapes, but she should really do an album with him." JIM

"**W**hen my kid was born I became, almost overnight, much more politically determined. Because you do become more responsible." JIM

"**B**efore the birth of my daughter, I used to care about things. But now I absolutely demand to know things! What does this mean, what does that mean? What will happen if this law is changed, or that law is passed? Because I'm aware now that I'm responsible for someone else, whereas before, I'd just say it was futile. I have to listen, I have to know." JIM

"**I**'m not sure I'd want to take credit for any of the stands we've made because, in many ways we've been forced into taking a stand on various issues. Kids started coming to gigs and asking questions of us – much more pertinent than 'Where do you get your hair cut?' No, our audiences were asking, 'Who's your God?', 'Who's your politician?', and 'Who's your hero?' They were forcing us into a corner, and that's what we needed." JIM

" *I* *like to try to fight pressure with pressure – by looking at someone else's*
pressure. I'm not trying to be Mr Humble, but I look at some guy in Glasgow,
with two kids at school and he hasn't got a job, and Christmas is coming up . . .
that's pressure. On a one-to-one level I can't really do anything about that, 'cos
he's still not the worst-off guy in the world, is he? He doesn't get the shit beaten
out of him by some secret police. So I feel for him, and I can associate myself
closer with him than someone in a jail in Argentina but, when it comes to actual
physical help, I'd rather help the guy in Argentina." JIM

" *W* *hen we started off, there was no political feeling whatsoever – on our*
first few records we're like voyeurs, watching and noting things down.
Now we're really throwing ourselves in. It's not because we think we know all
the answers, but just that we've learned much more in the past two or three
years. We're much more aware of our position, in as much as the amount of
people who buy our records and who come and see us, and that it's time to use
that power to a positive end. We're in this position, and we've got to try to do
something with it." JIM

" *W* *e're quite careerist really. We knew we wanted to tour in 1986 and then*
try to take a year off, but we also want to excel as songwriters. I'm not
interested in cultivating a status as the biggest band in the world, or even
building an army of fans. I like it the way it is now, where we've got these fans.
You can't spot them walking down the street but, they're always there." JIM

january

Simple Minds line-up alongside The Pretenders and UB40 for Brazil's spectacular 'Rock In Rio' event.

april

Confirmation arrives that one of Amnesty's nominated prisoners has been released — as a direct result of Simple Minds' efforts! At last year's San Diego show, Jim had made a passionate plea for a Tamil prisoner, P Udoyarajan, who had been detained for three years in Sri Lanka without charge or trial. Influenced by the band's concern, members of the audience later sent cards to the captors, who became so unnerved by the attention, that they subsequently released their detainee.

may

'In The City Of Light', the group's much mooted and long-awaited live album, finally sees the light of day. Naturally it goes straight to the top of the UK charts and, in so doing, becomes the fastest selling live album of all time. Ostensibly a souvenir of their 85/86 world tour, it does include one or two 'creative' overdubs however. Most interesting perhaps, is Derek Forbes' involvement in helping to remix the live version of 'Someone Somewhere (In Summertime)', for which he fails to receive a credit.

june

Plucked from the live album, 'Promised You A Miracle' is released as a single. Simple Minds make personal appearances in record shops, using traditional signing sessions as a further opportunity to promote Amnesty International. Everyone who gets Jim's signature, also leaves with a white postcard addressed to His Excellency PW Botha, State President of South Africa (as he was then).

july

Working on ideas individually a lot of the time, the band prepare melodies and riffs for some new material. They're also kept busy overseeing the development of their *own* studio at Loch Earn in the Central Highlands.

august

A period of self-reflection, as the band — Jim especially — ease back into home-life, *and* the Scottish community. This proves particularly problematical for the singer, whose wife is reluctant to leave London.

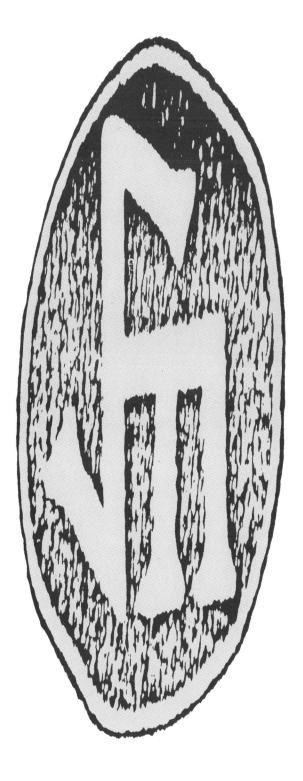

december

Simple Minds play three charity shows at Glasgow's Barrowland Ballroom. All profits go to Radio Clyde's 'Cash For Kids' appeal.

" *In The City Of Light' could well mark the end of an era for us . . . I really wouldn't be surprised if we came back with a whole different slant on things. It's the first real break we've had for nine years, so I suppose it's a sabbatical in some sense. It's very natural for us to feel that a door is closing, and that we're going to take a step on the outside and think.*" JIM

" *We've never played the game. Especially me and Charlie. I still can't believe it's me standing in the same room as Bruce Springsteen. There really is something about him y'know. To be as massive as he is, yet to be so unaffected. He's as big as Prince, or Elvis, or John Lennon, and they all went a bit mad. I think it's his upbringing that helps keep him sane. He's been such a source of inspiration to me. Even though he's way above me, I feel a kinship with him, he's so inarticulate. It's all inside, all heart. And then I meet Jack Nicholson, y'know, and everyone stands around being very cool, pretending they haven't noticed him. I go up to him and say, 'You're a fucking legend!' Like I say to Kenny Dalglish, 'I think you're fucking brilliant.' And you're not supposed to behave like that. But I don't give a fuck. It'll be the greatness of us, and the death of us too. We don't know how to behave.*" JIM

" *I think it's important to see the world as two ways of thinking . . . It's come through to me by travelling. I'm not aware of anyone lying in the street starving in Scotland yet. I've been to India, to the third world, and seen the tin shacks. I do feel patriotic, and I do feel close to Scotland – but then I don't. It's not that I don't give a toss, it's just that I can't afford to give a toss. I deal with my instinct, and then I try to articulate why I feel that way, and that leaves me in a position of hoping that maybe people around will see it in the same way and agree.*" JIM

" *Basically we had the year off. We'd worked more or less constantly for the last 10 years and we needed a break, not just in the physical sense, but also in a spiritual sense. We needed to get inspired again, to get back to an idea of real life, to get back to Scotland and be with friends and families, to take a step outside, keep check and put our feet back on the ground. And also to get hungry for it again.*" JIM

" *I'm not saying that you have to compromise in America, but you just get on with dealing with the fact that corruption is there. You have one foot on the inside and one on the outside – beat it at its own game. It's more exciting than asking whether your record company's taken John Peel out for a curry, just to get your record played that week. I'm talking about people meeting in Cleveland, and swapping a small paper bag that decides whether your record gets played. You can't take these people on.*" JIM

" *When you're successful, suddenly you're given all this space in the media to talk about yourselves, and flog the new album. Or, you can try to say that bit extra. I love the idea of rock music as fantastic entertainment, something that can move and uplift. But it's got to say something too. It's all part of becoming a dad as well. You start thinking about the world after you leave it. It's made me more determined. Instead of seeing something on the news and thinking, 'That's a drag,' I now try to think about what I might be able to do to change it.*" JIM

" *I've been a member of Amnesty International for years. On the odd Sunday afternoon you sit down and write these letters to governments and feel good for the rest of the week. It's a wee bit white, middle-class, guilt-ridden, but it seems to fit the lyrics.*" JIM

" *People tell me we're just using Amnesty, that it's just part of the image-building process. And I suppose there's a sense in which it is. I don't want to be seen to be in the same game as Billy Idol.*" JIM

" *It's nice to be able to actually do something positive about the problem of political prisoners, rather than just talk about it. We're sort of ambassadors, messengers if you like. My dad was a member when I was younger, and we've always tried to talk about freedom in our songs – and we've just taken it from there.*" JIM

" *I don't feel British at all. I don't blame anyone who leaves the country . . . I felt much better in America. It's so vulgar there, it's almost heartening. As soon as you realise how vulgar and corrupt it is, you just get on with the job. You grow up a lot – just inside the period of a week – when people tell you how it works over there.*" JIM

january

Simple Minds visit South America once again, and headline a pair of Brazilian open air events, in Rio de Janeiro and São Paulo.

february

A busy period of writing and rehearsing, as recording schedules start to be planned. Producers Trevor Horn and Stephen Lipson join the group in their newly acquired Highland studio complex – set within a converted Victorian mansion.

june

Simple Minds appear at a star-studded Wembley Stadium show to mark the 70th birthday of the imprisoned African Rights leader, Nelson Mandela. The band's 'Mandela Day' is written especially for the occasion, and further reflects their commitment to basic human rights campaigns. Peter Gabriel joins the band on stage for an emotive rendition of the anthemic 'Biko'. It's Simple Minds' only live show of the year.

july

Rumours of a break-up in Jim's marriage begin to spread.

september

The band spend increasingly lengthy periods in the studio, as they begin to politicise their work a lot more. This it seems, is partly to satisfy their own social consciences, and partly to entertain other peoples'.

PETER Gabriel and Jim Kerr join forces on the inspirational chant 'Biko'.

" **I**f any band was thinking of going for the big league, I would thoroughly advocate it – if they have that urge. See if you can get to the back of the Hope And Anchor. The back of The Marquee. The back of The Lyceum. The back of Hammersmith Odeon. The back of Wembley Arena. Then the back of Wembley Stadium. When I talked to Bono about it, he reckoned that Wembley Stadium was too big. I thought about it all the time. We went on stage at the Mandela concert, and I was still thinking about it. We went straight into 'Waterfront', restrained I might add, and I thought you fuckers, it's too small! It was all right. I knew the song had a heart big enough for the place. I knew that people at the back were getting it, and they did get it!" JIM

FORMER Smiths guitarist
Johnny Marr joins Simple
Minds at London's Wembley
Stadium as part of the Mandela
Day event. Far right: with
Little Steven.

"*I suddenly felt useless living by proxy . . . I started thinking about responsibilities to friends and family. I realised I had to stop and put everything in order. So we turned our backs on the whole thing for a while. It gave us strength and a certain peace of mind. When you're on the road for 14 months, you end up shirking a lot of responsibilities. I realised that, in certain respects, I was becoming ruthless.*" JIM

"*When Jerry Dammers got in touch with us to do the Mandela Day concert, the idea was not just to play, but to have a varied set and special guests. Everyone was supposed to write a song specifically for the day, which I thought was a great idea, but we were the only ones who did! Beyond that, not many people did relevant songs that would have focused the protest.*" JIM

"*When we were in London recently, we had a couple of black guys come up and say, 'Brilliant, how are you doing?' We hardly get recognised by anyone, especially in London, but getting involved in 'Mandela Day' obviously meant a lot to them, and that was great.*" CHARLIE

"*I remember when we did the Amnesty shows, we left leaflets on chairs to tell people what was going on, real idiot-board tactics, and we would come out of the gig feeling great, as if the roof was gonna come down. Then we would see that the pamphlets had been made into paper aeroplanes, and were strewn all over the place. Your own voice starts asking if you're mad, if you're just wasting your time. But then you find that people have been given their freedom, partly because of our actions. Amnesty went on record about that. It just gives you the encouragement to do more. It shows what can happen when you apply yourself.*" JIM

" *When I'm asked who my heroes are, rather than saying Lou Reed or Bob Dylan – which goes without saying – I say Amnesty International.*" JIM

" *We bought this Victorian place . . . but we only got permission from the local authorities to convert it into a studio for our sole use. They were a wee bit nervous about us, and I can see why. It really didn't bother us, because we didn't want to spend millions on a state-of-the-art affair, which we'd have to rent out to break even – ripping our hair out if it wasn't going well – and not being able to use it if it was booked solid. As a joke we christened the place, 'Bonnie Wee Studios', and record companies have been phoning up in all seriousness saying, 'Is that Bonnie Wee Studios?' It's difficult to keep a straight face.*" JIM

" *Having made our base back here, you become aware of the pain that a lot of people are feeling in Scotland, especially after the last few years. Nationalism isn't really it . . . Since I've come back I've travelled a lot in my own country, and I've read the history. We built the studio in the country. I know that sounds kind of hippy-ish, but it's glorious, the whole drama of the place . . . In a nutshell it became apparent that this was our spiritual home, and the strength we get here – on an artistic and personal level – we just don't get any place else.*" JIM

" *There's a difference between being an integral member of Simple Minds and just being a member – you live it. But Mel lives in London and is very much a London boy, and I think he's got a circle of friends who fill his head with a load of rubbish – and he knows I think that. But on stage he's fantastic.*" JIM

JIM'S estranged wife also
joined in the day long
celebrations. Chrissie on stage
with Ali Campbell of UB40.

february

Simple Minds return with a new EP entitled 'Ballad Of The Streets'. Featuring both 'Mandela Day' and a cover of Peter Gabriel's 'Biko', it's the new song 'Belfast Child' that earns most of the airplay. Based on the traditional Irish folk song, 'She Moved Through The Fair', some broadcasting executives try to ignore it at first, but public demand makes *that* a little difficult. 'Ballad Of The Streets' goes to number one, and stays there for a month!

march

The break-up of Jim's marriage becomes public knowledge, and plans are made for a divorce later in the year.

april

A follow-up single, 'This Is Your Land', fails to repeat the EP's success, and disappears quicker than you can say 'Where's the new album then?'

may

'Street Fighting Years' reaches the shops, and is generally considered their finest LP to date. Retaining all the power of 'Once Upon A Time', the band finally come up with material to match the mood — a string of songs that are worth being powerful about. Other musicians on the LP include drummers Stewart Copeland and Manu Katche, along with violinist Lisa Germano. Lou Reed also appears in a cameo capacity on one track, 'This Is Your Land'.

Simple Minds deny media rumours that Mel Gaynor has been sacked from the group, and prove it when Mel teams up with them for the start of a 16-month world tour in Italy. By now, the only man missing from the *last* touring line-up, is bassist John Giblin. He's been replaced by one-time Pretender, Malcolm Foster. The stage band is also augmented by Lisa Germano (who last toured with John Cougar Mellencamp) and singer Annie McCraig.

Opening dates in Florence, are followed by shows in Modena, Milan and Rome. The busy month comes to a close with three French shows at Fréjus, Lyons and Toulouse.

june

The European trek continues with dates in Bordeaux, Nantes, Brest, Brussels, Stockholm, Copenhagen, Hamburg, Berlin, Dortmund, Cologne, Paris, Oldenburg, Frankfurt, Mannheim, Stuttgart, Munich . . .

july

. . . Konstanz, Zurich, Avignon, Madrid, Barcelona, Rotterdam and, at long last, Leeds and London where they perform at Wembley Stadium.

august

More UK dates, this time in Birmingham, Cardiff, Edinburgh, London, with Dublin to follow in Ireland. The band insist on changing the Edinburgh venue from Murrayfield to Meadowbank, following an anti-apartheid row with the ground's administrators, the Scottish Rugby Union.
'Kick It In' is released, and subsequently ignored by all and sundry.

september

Simple Minds interrupt further European commitments, to play three extra shows in Birmingham.

october

The band finally leave these shores and disappear into the sunset. An ensuing string of overseas dates is expected to be their last for almost 12 months, when it's anticipated they will again visit America.

december

In the meantime Simple Minds bring the decade to a close with the surprise release of their 'Amsterdam EP', which includes a version of Prince's classic, 'Sign O' The Times'. While critics question the road ahead for nineties rock, Simple Minds are already on it. And with studio time booked for the New Year, the band seem likely to be setting the standard for a good few years to come . . .

" *We didn't have any choice but to be vulgarised by America. But that's why we came back to Scotland. The values that we were brought up with are still intact. If they go out the window for a while, we come back here and they come back into focus again. It exists whether we exist or not. We won't change it, we just have to deal with it. If there is such a thing as a big league, we want to be in it.*" JIM

" *My break-up with Chrissie put everything in perspective. When it came to the pain, I had a choice. I could have given the band up, to keep the family unit together . . . Don't think I didn't consider it. For a few months it was first and foremost in my mind. Then I began to think about the fact that I'd been writing since I was the smallest kid. I'd known Charlie Burchill since I was eight-years-old. Simple Minds had been through ups and downs but had come through. We'd come a long way. I knew I couldn't opt out of that!*" JIM

" *Chrissie and I spent too long away from each other. Love, marriage, it needs watering every day. Otherwise it just dies.*" JIM

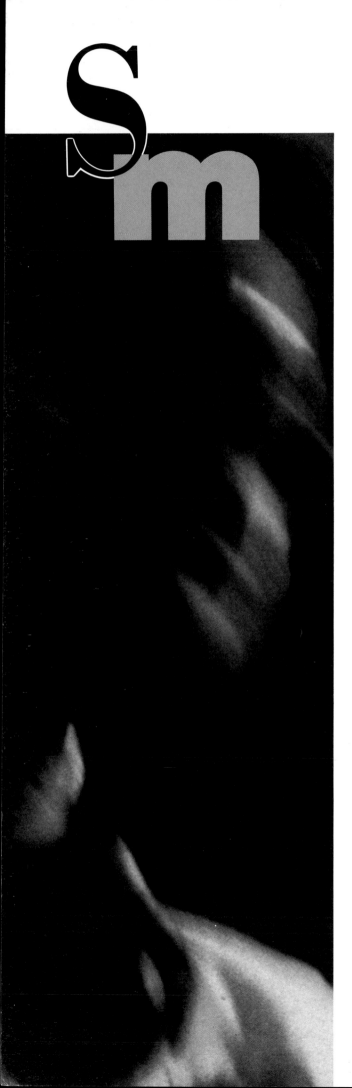

" It's Chrissie I have to thank for getting me to stop eating meat. I'm now vegetarian, and a lot happier for it." JIM

" I'm not interested in giving a tenner to this, or 10 grand to that, but I find the idea of writing a song fantastic and challenging. It's like Victor Jara said, you can cage a singer but you can't cage the song. Songs live on – people learn them and pass them on." JIM

" First and foremost, what we're doing is entertainment, but entertainment doesn't have to be hollow or vacuous. The best entertainment I can think of has always been illuminated and articulated, right through Berthold Brecht, Jacques Brel, or the Spanish poets during the revolution. These people could articulate something in a nutshell and still make it entertaining." JIM

" Our new songs reflect the chaos of this day and age, and the album is called 'Street Fighting Years' because they're all about some kind of conflict." JIM

" It's very hard for me to see any logical connection between 'Once Upon A Time' and this, 'Street Fighting Years'. It just feels such a world away. The progress is still intrinsic, and it still has the spirit of life that our music has had for the past six or seven years, but this is a whole new thing. And it's probably got to do with time, living away from it, being in Scotland, recording differently." JIM

" In 10 years of writing, we've written one song that I think is overtly political, and that's 'Mandela Day'. Every other song, even 'Belfast Child', is about people and places. 'Belfast Child' is a political song only because it has the word 'Belfast' in the title. I mean, the song is about somebody who's not on any side, who's lived there for 20 years, who's trying to live from day to day, and who doesn't have any faith in either side." JIM

" When we put out 'Belfast Child' everybody said, 'Phew, you've been away for three-and-a-half years and you're putting out this folk song? It's got no beat, lasts for six minutes, and Radio One with this whole broadcasting thing about songs mentioning the Irish situation . . . Suicide.' And y'know, I was really hoping that, if we ever had a number one, it would be with this one . . . I just feel dead encouraged." JIM

" A Glaswegian boy writing about Belfast . . .? Well, The Band, one of the greatest groups ever, they wrote the perfect song about the deep South – 'The Night They Drove Old Dixie Down' – yet they were from Canada. It sometimes works better if you're writing from the outside, if you're not entrenched in it. And Belfast is only about 60 miles from Glasgow, it's part of us." JIM

" In 'Belfast Child', I was also trying to express the way I felt about a friend who was killed in Glasgow about a year-and-a-half ago, as a result – I suppose you could say – of urban madness, or urban confusion. He was 19. He was actually my brother's best friend, and his older brother was a close friend of mine. He went to a party in a rather dubious area of Glasgow and a fight started. He wasn't the type to be involved, so he grabbed his girlfriend and headed for the door to get out. But there were three guys, really high on glue,

with knives and they just set on him and didn't stop. And just like that he was gone. The kids who did it were between 15 and 18. They were the types who probably never left Glasgow, who've probably never seen any countryside, who've probably experienced nothing other than a broken-down city, living with drunken parents and surrounded by all this urban madness and energy – the same as hundreds of thousands of other kids in all the major cities around the world. And I didn't feel, nor did his brother feel, any desire for revenge. There was just a void, and a question, why? Just why? . . . I'm really haunted by that, and the theme crops up in various ways on the album." JIM

"We decided to do the video for 'Belfast Child' actually in Belfast, because it would have been a cop-out not to. At first we were against it, because the last thing we want to do is to exploit it, or have pictures of us looking like The Clash, standing at the barricades and then fucking off back home." JIM

"It's great to write a song which takes an idea and hits the nail on the head in three minutes, even if it doesn't explain things in detail, but nods to what's goin' on. That Prince song, 'Sign O' The Times' is a great example. He summed up the month it was released, and there was still room for romance at the end. It was fucking brilliant! . . . Everyone wants to write something timeless, but you run the risk of ending up with 'Nights In White Satin'." JIM

"The important factor for us, is that there should still be a challenge. The only parallel I can make with the music is, like, if you were a kid and you were locked in this room, and that's all you know. You're growing up, feeling yourself getting bigger, and you think you know the whole world. And then you come to the window, look out, and see this whole view that you haven't got a clue about . . . Now, I don't want to get out of the room necessarily, but I do want us to understand, and learn about what's outside it." JIM

"You don't suddenly stop making good records 'cos you reach a certain age . . . Who's making Lou Reed useless in 1989? Nobody. Who's to say that Paul McCartney hasn't got a classic song coming up? . . . That kind of thing is outdated. That is a dinosaur attitude. I would hate to feel anyone thought that we were it, the experienced wise men, the veterans of whatever. When I meet a Van Morrison, or a Lou Reed, I just feel completely wet behind the ears. An apprentice." JIM

"I came across Lou Reed in Dublin playing with U2. We'd done a version of his 'Street Hassle' (on 'Sparkle In The Rain'), which everyone hated apart from Lou Reed! So I met him, and was amazed how lucid and enthusiastic he was . . . But we still didn't really expect him to come and sing on our record. We got a tape to him though, which he said he liked, and the next thing we knew he was in the studio with us. He said, 'What exactly are you looking for here,' and I said I wanted him to do a parody of Lou Reed. 'Well,' he drawled, 'everyone else is doing that, so why shouldn't I?'" JIM

"The other night I was swinging the microphone around my head. Real Roger Daltrey! It got to about a radius of 16 feet when I thought, 'Hey, this could be dangerous.' And just at that moment it swung round and whacked me in the face. If the humiliation hadn't hurt so much it would have killed me. The roadies say I should try something safer . . . like soap on a rope." JIM

" *I don't want to be a voyeur or a fly on the wall any more. I have no time for it now. I want to be in the middle throwing punches. Robert Smith's been giving me a hard time about being more successful than he is, or something . . . but times change, y'know? Robert's thirty-something and he's still writing songs about being eaten by spiders.*" JIM

" *The British government is, perhaps, the biggest ally that the South African régime has. We really must stand up and say that this isn't on . . . because the black people have their backs so much against the wall, they're being forced to act in whatever way they can. And although I'd rather they didn't use violence, who am I to say they shouldn't.*" JIM

" *People make a big thing of the fact that I don't live in Glasgow any more . . . They say, 'Ah, you're away living in that Edinburgh,' as if it's fucking Tasmania! I mean, for fuck's sake! My parents are in Glasgow, all my friends are there. I haven't left Glasgow. It's only 35 minutes away!*" JIM

" *I can't really say what Edinburgh's like . . . I don't go out there much. I'm not part of any scene. I haven't got many friends there. I never go to any clubs. I s'pose Edinburgh's just quaint. It's quaint and you can't get parked.*" JIM

" *We are Scots. But right now there's a real crying out generally for much more of a national identity, and I think that's a cul-de-sac. I've seen no vision in it at all, apart from just anti-Englishness, and who cares about that? That's just a chip on the shoulder.*" JIM

" *When we were sitting at number one, our (footballing) hero Maurice Johnston left us some tickets for the Scotland versus France match, and we were really hyped up about this game. We were driving to Hampden and, 20 minutes before the kick-off, I suddenly had a blow-out on my tyre. We thought we'd had it. And then Charlie and I just looked at each other and said, 'Well, let's thumb it again.' So there we were, number one, and thumbing a lift at Harthill in the pouring rain. This guy stopped and he was going, 'Jim, Jim! Are you gonna sign this?' And I was going, 'Are you on your way to Hampden?' Ha! His girlfriend was not amused. He said he wasn't going there, and we said, 'Oh yes you are!' He got us there in lightning speed with a minute to go. And we won. And we thought, it's great being in Simple Minds!*" JIM

" *What I'm writing now is an honest response to what I see going on around me, and probably there is a feeling of guilt there. You see events from 30, 40 or 50 years ago and you think, 'Why did people let that go on, why didn't they do something about it?' I can imagine in years to come my kids asking me about South Africa or Central America, and screaming at me, 'You had the chance to rock the boat, you could have done something in your own way!' . . . I began thinking more and more about it, and now I think that writing a song is equivalent to throwing a stone. I think stone-throwing is good 'cos – as much as causes like Amnesty are all about peace and non-violence – I'm running out of patience. For me, the song should be a weapon.*" JIM

" *At the end of the day we are a hell of a noise, and it's gonna get out of hand sometimes, and then it's gonna be really good. It's very simple really. You get obsessed with all the technicalities, and whether this stands for this or whether the record company hyped that, but there's only two types of music, and that's good and bad.*" JIM

singles

Johnny And The Self Abusers

SAINTS AND SINNERS/DEAD VANDALS
Chiswick NS 22. November 1977.

Simple Minds

LIFE IN A DAY/SPECIAL VIEW
Zoom ZUM 10. April 1979.

CHELSEA GIRL/GARDEN OF HATE
Zoom ZUM 11. June 1979.

CHANGELING/PREMONITION
Arista ARIST 325. February 1980.

I TRAVEL/NEW WARM SKIN
Arista ARIST 372. September
1980.
(Initial copies include blue flexi
single KALEIDOSCOPE/FILM THEME
DUB)

I TRAVEL/FILM THEME
Arista 12-inch ARIST 12372.
September 1980.

CELEBRATE/CHANGELING/I TRAVEL
Arista ARIST 394. April 1981.

CELEBRATE/CHANGELING/I TRAVEL
Arista 12-inch ARIST 12394.
April 1981.

THE AMERICAN/LEAGUE OF NATIONS
Virgin VS 410. May 1981.

THE AMERICAN/LEAGUE OF NATIONS
Virgin 12-inch VS 410-12.
May 1981.

**LOVE SONG/THIS EARTH THAT YOU
WALK UPON**
Virgin VS 434. August 1981.

**LOVE SONG/THIS EARTH THAT YOU
WALK UPON**
Virgin 12-inch VS 434-12.
August 1981.

**SWEAT IN BULLET/20TH CENTURY
PROMISED LAND**
Virgin VS 451. November 1981.

**SWEAT IN BULLET/20TH CENTURY
PROMISED LAND/PREMONITION/IN
TRANCE AS MISSION**
Virgin double pack VS 451.
November 1981.

**SWEAT IN BULLET/20TH CENTURY
PROMISED LAND/LEAGUE OF NATIONS
(LIVE)/IN TRANCE AS MISSION**
Virgin 12-inch VS 451-12.
November 1981.

I TRAVEL/THIRTY FRAMES A SECOND
Arista ARIST 448. January 1982.

**I TRAVEL/THIRTY FRAMES A SECOND/
I TRAVEL (LIVE)**
Arista 12-inch ARIST 12448.
January 1982.

**PROMISED YOU A MIRACLE/THEME
FROM GREAT CITIES**
Virgin VS 488. April 1982.

**PROMISED YOU A MIRACLE/THEME
FROM GREAT CITIES/SEEING OUT
THE ANGEL**
Virgin 12-inch VS 488-12.
April 1982.

GLITTERING PRIZE/GLITTERING THEME
Virgin VS 511. August 1982.

**GLITTERING PRIZE (CLUB MIX)/
GLITTERING THEME**
Virgin 12-inch VS 511-12.
August 1982.

**SOMEONE SOMEWHERE IN
SUMMERTIME/KING IS WHITE AND IN
THE CROWD**
Virgin poster sleeve VS 538.
November 1982.

**SOMEONE SOMEWHERE IN
SUMMERTIME/KING IS WHITE AND IN
THE CROWD**
Virgin picture disc VS 538.
November 1982.

**SOMEONE SOMEWHERE IN
SUMMERTIME/KING IS WHITE AND IN
THE CROWD/EVERY HEAVEN**
Virgin 12-inch VS 538-12.
November 1982.

I TRAVEL/FILM THEME
Virgin 12-inch VS 578-12.
April 1983.

**WATERFRONT/HUNTER AND THE
HUNTED**
Virgin VS 636. November 1983.

**WATERFRONT/HUNTER AND THE
HUNTED/IF YOU WANT MY LOVE**
Virgin 12-inch VS 636-12.
November 1983.

SPEED YOUR LOVE TO ME/BASS LINE
Virgin VS 649. January 1984.

SPEED YOUR LOVE TO ME/BASS LINE
Virgin picture disc VS 649.
January 1984.

SPEED YOUR LOVE TO ME/BASS LINE
Virgin 12-inch VS 649-12.
January 1984.

**UP ON THE CATWALK/A BRASS BAND
IN AFRICA**
Virgin VS 661. March 1984.

**UP ON THE CATWALK/A BRASS BAND
IN AFRICA**
Virgin picture disc VS 661.
March 1984.

**UP ON THE CATWALK/A BRASS BAND
IN AFRICAN CHIMES**
Virgin 12-inch VS 661-12.
March 1984.

DON'T YOU FORGET ABOUT ME/
A BRASS BAND IN AFRICA
Virgin VS 749. April 1985.

DON'T YOU FORGET ABOUT ME/
A BRASS BAND IN AFRICA
Virgin shaped picture disc VS 749.
April 1985.

DON'T YOU FORGET ABOUT ME/
A BRASS BAND IN AFRICAN CHIMES
Virgin 12-inch VS 749-12.
April 1985.

ALIVE AND KICKING/INSTRUMENTAL
Virgin VS 817. September 1985.

ALIVE AND KICKING/DUB VERSION
Virgin 12-inch VS 817-12.
September 1985.

ALIVE AND KICKING/UP ON THE
CATWALK (LIVE)
Virgin 12-inch VS 817-13.
September 1985.

SANCTIFY YOURSELF/INSTRUMENTAL
Virgin SM 1. January 1986.

SANCTIFY YOURSELF
Virgin double pack EP SMP 1.
January 1986.

SANCTIFY YOURSELF (EXTENDED)/
SANCTIFY YOURSELF (DUB MIX)
Virgin 12-inch SM 112.
January 1986.

ALL THE THINGS SHE SAID/DON'T YOU
(FORGET ABOUT ME) (LIVE)
Virgin VS 860. March 1986.

ALL THE THINGS SHE SAID/DON'T YOU
(FORGET ABOUT ME) (LIVE)/PROMISED
YOU A MIRACLE (US REMIX)
Virgin 12-inch VS 860-12.
March 1986.

GHOSTDANCING/JUNGLELAND
Virgin VS 907. November 1986.

GHOSTDANCING (EXT)/INSTRUMENTAL/
JUNGLELAND (EXT)/INSTRUMENTAL
Virgin 12-inch VS 907-12.
November 1986.

GHOSTDANCING (EXT)/INSTRUMENTAL/
JUNGLELAND (EXT)/INSTRUMENTAL
Virgin CD MIKE 907-12.
November 1986.

PROMISED YOU A MIRACLE (LIVE)/
BOOK OF BRILLIANT THINGS (LIVE)
Virgin SM 2. June 1987.

PROMISED YOU A MIRACLE (LIVE)/
BOOK OF BRILLIANT THINGS (LIVE)
Virgin 10-inch SM 210. June 1987.

PROMISED YOU A MIRACLE (LIVE)/
BOOK OF BRILLIANT THINGS (LIVE)/
GLITTERING PRIZE (LIVE)/CELEBRATION
(LIVE)
Virgin 12-inch SM 212. June 1987.

PROMISED YOU A MIRACLE (LIVE)/
BOOK OF BRILLIANT THINGS (LIVE)/
GLITTERING PRIZE (LIVE)/CELEBRATION
(LIVE)
Virgin cassette SMC 212.
June 1987.

BALLAD OF THE STREETS: BELFAST
CHILD/MANDELA DAY/BIKO
Virgin EP SM 3. February 1989.

BALLAD OF THE STREETS: BELFAST
CHILD/MANDELA DAY/BIKO
Virgin double-pack EP SMX 3.
February 1989.

BALLAD OF THE STREETS: BELFAST
CHILD/MANDELA DAY/BIKO
Virgin EP box set SMXB 3.
February 1989.

BALLAD OF THE STREETS: BELFAST
CHILD/MANDELA DAY/BIKO
Virgin EP cassette SMXC 3.
February 1989.

BALLAD OF THE STREETS: BELFAST
CHILD (FULL-LENGTH MIX)/MANDELA
DAY/BIKO
Virgin EP 12-inch SMXT 3.
February 1989.

BALLAD OF THE STREETS: BELFAST
CHILD (FULL-LENGTH MIX)/MANDELA
DAY/BIKO
Virgin EP 5-inch CD SMXCD 3.
February 1989.

THIS IS YOUR LAND/SATURDAY GIRL
Virgin SM 4. April 1989.

THIS IS YOUR LAND/SATURDAY GIRL/
YEAR OF THE DRAGON
Virgin 3-inch CD SMXCD 4.
April 1989.

THIS IS YOUR LAND/SATURDAY GIRL/
YEAR OF THE DRAGON
Virgin 12-inch SMXT 4. April 1989.

THIS IS YOUR LAND/SATURDAY GIRL/
YEAR OF THE DRAGON
Virgin 12-inch gatefold sleeve
SMXTG 4. April 1989.

KICK IT IN/WATERFRONT (89 REMIX)
Virgin SMX 5. July 1989.

KICK IT IN/WATERFRONT (89 REMIX)/
BIG SLEEP (LIVE)
Virgin 12-inch SMXT 5. July 1989.

KICK IT IN/WATERFRONT (89 REMIX)/
BIG SLEEP (LIVE)
Virgin 3-inch CD SMXCD 5.
July 1989.

KICK IT IN/WATERFRONT (89 REMIX)/
BIG SLEEP (LIVE)
Virgin cassette SMXC 5. July 1989.

THE AMSTERDAM EP: SIGN O' THE
TIMES (EDIT)/LET IT ALL COME DOWN
(EDIT)/ JERUSALEM
Virgin SMX6. November 1989.

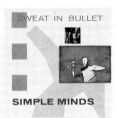

THE AMSTERDAM EP: LET IT ALL COME DOWN/SIGN O' THE TIMES/JERUSALEM
Virgin 12-inch SMXT6.
November 1989.

THE AMSTERDAM EP: SIGN O' THE TIMES (EDIT)/LET IT ALL COME DOWN (EDIT)/JERUSALEM
Virgin cassette single SMXC6.
November 1989.

THE AMSTERDAM EP: LET IT ALL COME DOWN/SIGN O' THE TIMES/JERUSALEM
Virgin 3-inch CD SMXCD6.
November 1989.

THE AMSTERDAM EP: SIGN O' THE TIMES/LET IT ALL COME DOWN/ SIGN O' THE TIMES (EDIT)/JERUSALEM
Virgin 5-inch CD SMXX6.
November 1989.

albums

LIFE IN A DAY
Someone/Life In A Day/Sad Affair/
All For You/Pleasantly Disturbed/
No Cure/Chelsea Girl/Wasteland/
Destiny/Murder Story.
Zoom ZULP 1. July 1979.

REAL TO REAL CACOPHONY
Real To Real/Naked Eye/Citizen
(Dance Of Youth)/Carnival (Shelter
In A Suitcase)/Factory/Cacophony/
Veldt/Premonition/Changeling/
Film Theme/Calling Your Name/
Scar.
Arista SPART 1109. January 1980.

EMPIRES AND DANCE
I Travel/Today I Died Again/
Celebrate/This Fear Of Gods/
Capital City/Constantinople Line/
Twist-Run-Repulsion/Thirty Frames
A Second/Kant-Kino/Room.
Arista SPART 1140.
September 1980.

SONS AND FASCINATION/SISTER FEELINGS CALL
Virgin double album set V 2207.
August 1981.

SONS AND FASCINATION
In Trance As Mission/Sweat In
Bullet/70 Cities As Love Brings The
Fall/Boys From Brazil/Love Song/
This Earth That You Walk Upon/
Sons And Fascination/Seeing Out
The Angel.
Virgin V 2207. September 1981.

SISTER FEELINGS CALL
Theme From Great Cities/The
American/20th Century Promised
Land/Wonderful In Young Life/
League Of Nations/Careful In
Career/Sound In 70 Cities.
Virgin OVED 2. October 1981.

CELEBRATION
Arista SPART 1183. February
1982.

**NEW GOLD DREAM
(81, 82, 83, 84)**
Someone Somewhere In
Summertime/Colours Fly And
Catherine Wheel/Promised You A
Miracle/Big Sleep/Somebody Up
There Likes Me/New Gold Dream
(81, 82, 83, 84)/Glittering Prize/
Hunter And The Hunted/King Is
White And In The Crowd.
Virgin V 2230. September 1982.

REAL TO REAL CACOPHONY
Virgin V 2246. October 1982.

EMPIRES AND DANCE
Virgin V 2247. October 1982.

CELEBRATION
Virgin V 2248. October 1982.

LIFE IN A DAY
Virgin VM 6. October 1982.

SPARKLE IN THE RAIN
Up On The Catwalk/Book Of
Brilliant Things/Speed Your Love
To Me/ Waterfront/East At Easter/
Street Hassle/White Hot Day/'C'
Moon Cry Like A Baby/The Kick
Inside Of Me/ Shake Off The
Ghosts.
Virgin V 2300. February 1984.

SPARKLE IN THE RAIN
Virgin white vinyl V 2300.
February 1984.

ONCE UPON A TIME
Once Upon A Time/All The Things
She Said/Ghost Dancing/Alive And
Kicking/Oh Jungleland/I Wish You
Were Here/Sanctify Yourself/Come
A Long Way.
Virgin V 2364. October 1985.

ONCE UPON A TIME
Virgin picture disc V 2364.
October 1985.

LIFE IN A DAY
Virgin OVED 95. October 1985.

REAL TO REAL CACOPHONY
Virgin OVED 124. October 1985.

EMPIRES AND DANCE
Virgin OVED 211. May 1987.

IN THE CITY OF LIGHT
Ghost Dancing/Big Sleep/
Waterfront/Promised You A
Miracle/ Someone Somewhere In
Summertime/Oh Jungleland/Alive
And Kicking/Don't You (Forget
About Me)/Once Upon A Time/Book
Of Brilliant Things/East At Easter/
Sanctify Yourself/Love Song/New
Gold Dream.
Virgin SMVL 1. May 1987.

IN THE CITY OF LIGHT
Virgin double album SMDLX 1.
May 1987.

INTERVIEW PICTURE DISC
Virgin Baktabak BAK 2070.
November 1987.

STREET FIGHTING YEARS
Street Fighting Years/Soul Crying
Out/Wall Of Love/This Is Your
Land/ Take A Step Back/Kick It In/
Let It All Come Down/Mandela
Day/Belfast Child/Biko/When
Spirits Rise.
Virgin MINDS 1. May 1989.

cds

NEW GOLD DREAM
Virgin CDV 2230. January 1983.

SPARKLE IN THE RAIN
Virgin CDV 2300. February 1984.

ONCE UPON A TIME
Virgin CDV 2364. November 1985.

REAL TO REAL CACOPHONY
Virgin CDV 2246. January 1986.

EMPIRES AND DANCE
Virgin CDV 2247. January 1986.

**SONS AND FASCINATION/SISTER
FEELINGS CALL**
Virgin CDV 2207. April 1986.

CELEBRATION
Virgin CDV 2207. January 1987.

IN THE CITY OF LIGHT
Virgin CDSM 1. May 1987.

LIFE IN A DAY
Virgin SMCD 6. July 1987.

STREET FIGHTING YEARS
Virgin MINDSCD1. May 1989.

STREET FIGHTING YEARS
Virgin SMBXD1. December 1989.
Limited edition numbered box set.
SMBXC1.

family tree

SIMPLE MINDS Mk 1.

January 1978 – February 1978

Jim KERR vocals, Charlie BURCHILL guitar, Brian McGEE drums, Duncan BARNWELL guitar, Tony DONALD bass, Mick MacNEIL keyboards.

SIMPLE MINDS Mk 2.

March 1978 – May 1978

Jim KERR vocals, Charlie BURCHILL guitar, Brian McGEE drums, Duncan BARNWELL guitar, Mick MacNEIL keyboards, Derek FORBES bass.

SIMPLE MINDS Mk 3.

June 1978 – July 1981

Jim KERR vocals, Charlie BURCHILL guitar, Brian McGEE drums, Mick MacNEIL keyboards, Derek FORBES bass.

SIMPLE MINDS Mk 4.

August 1981 – May 1982

Jim KERR vocals, Charlie BURCHILL guitar, Mick MacNEIL keyboards, Derek FORBES bass, Kenny HYSLOP drums.

SIMPLE MINDS Mk 5.

June 1982 – October 1982

Jim KERR vocals, Charlie BURCHILL guitar, Mick MacNEIL keyboards, Derek FORBES bass, Mike OGLETREE drums.

SIMPLE MINDS Mk 6.

November 1982 – March 1985

Jim KERR vocals, Charlie BURCHILL guitar, Mick MacNEIL keyboards, Derek FORBES bass, Mel GAYNOR drums.

SIMPLE MINDS Mk 7.

April 1985 – April 1989

Jim KERR vocals, Charlie BURCHILL guitar, Mick MacNEIL keyboards, Mel GAYNOR drums, John GIBLIN bass.

SIMPLE MINDS Mk 8.

May 1989 – time of writing

Jim KERR vocals, Charlie BURCHILL guitar, Mick MacNEIL keyboards, Mel GAYNOR drums, Malcolm FOSTER bass.